Eileen Aldridge

# Porcelain

illustrated by Peter Morter
& Design Bureau

**Paul Hamlyn · London**
Sun Books · Melbourne

# FOREWORD

In a lifetime of study one could not discover all there is to know on the subject of porcelain. Naturally an expert tends to specialise and, though he may be generally knowledgeable, it is in his own particular subject that he feels most confident. In the ever fascinating subject of porcelain there is always something more to learn as yet another new piece comes to light.

It is the intention of this small volume to introduce the reader to the mysteries of porcelain, from its earliest manufacture in China, to the discovery of its secrets in eighteenth-century Europe, and its eventual manufacture in the United States. I have given some account of the founding of each factory, its duration and its main characteristics and, wherever possible, named the most important artists known to be working there. Illustrations are fitted as closely to the text as possible.

The subject has produced a large literature. This brief, but I hope comprehensive, account is intended to lay the field before the reader and whet the appetite for further reading. It is obviously easier for the collector to find pieces from his own country and my advice would be to choose a factory which specially appeals, to visit the museums housing good collections and really familiarise oneself with the porcelain. However, it is difficult to gain a real guide to value from auctions as prices vary so much from sale to sale.

Eileen Aldridge

The illustrations on pages 68, 72, 73, 93, 110, 122, 124, 125, 130–137, 139 and 141 were copied from objects in the Victoria and Albert Museum. The publishers gratefully acknowledge the kind cooperation of the museum authorities.

Published by The Hamlyn Publishing Group Limited
London · New York · Sydney · Toronto
Hamlyn House, Feltham, Middlesex, England
In association with Sun Books Pty Melbourne

Second impression 1969.

Phototypeset by Oliver Burridge Filmsetting Limited, Crawley, Sussex
Colour separations by Schwitter Limited, Zurich
Printed in England by Sir Joseph Causton & Sons Limited

# CONTENTS

## INTRODUCTION

The origins of porcelain were founded in the early vitreous stoneware of the Chinese Han dynasty, some 200 years BC. It was nearly a thousand years later that a translucent porcelain was made and considerably longer before the production of the ceramics which were the wonder and the envy of the Western world.

The principal ingredients of Chinese porcelain were a white china-clay known as kaolin, and petuntse, a feldspathic rock which becomes vitreous when fired at about 1450 degrees centigrade. This produced a hard-paste porcelain, the glaze for which was also feldspathic and was usually fired in one with the body, becoming an integral part of it. The fusion made for perfection of surface; glazing on already biscuited hard-paste produced a minutely pitted surface, referred to as 'chicken-skin' when found on Chinese porcelain.

Soft-paste porcelain was a mixture of a white clay and a ground glassy substance. In England a natural mixture of china-clay and steatite was found in soap rock. The glaze, added at the second firing which was lower in temperature than the first, was on top of the paste, not fused with it, and this sometimes caused crazing, especially when the addition of lead made it run and pool in the hollows.

An ability to recognise hard-paste from soft-paste is of first importance to the collector. If a file is used on the base of hard-paste it will seldom make an impression, but the method is a ruthless one which leaves the piece scarred if it proves to be soft-paste after all. The latter suffers more damage through time and often shows a maze of fine scratching and rubbing on the parts most exposed to use and handling. A chip in hard-paste reveals a break such as one might see in a piece of thick glass, sometimes described as colloidal. A chip in soft-paste shows a granular surface, a refined version of what one would see in broken earthenware.

It is said that Marco Polo brought the first porcelain back to Europe and filled the heads of kings and alchemists with dreams of discovering its secrets. Its fragile translucent beauty made it eminently desirable, and it was accorded an esteem usually reserved for silver and gold and frequently took their place as a presentation gift from one royal court to another.

By the beginning of the eighteenth century many attempts had been made to find a formula and alchemists and potters had been imprisoned with a royal command to succeed on pain of death. This encouragement seemed to produce results since it was under these circumstances that Böttger eventually produced a type of porcelain for Augustus the Strong. It did not, however, induce loyalty in the workers and the secrets were eventually spread through Europe by renegade craftsmen.

Though the earliest porcelain emulated the Chinese and Japanese wares and some work continued to be done in that style, it was not long before a European character began to assert itself in both form and decoration. Designers turned to their native silverware and metalwork for inspiration and subjects were adapted from paintings and engravings.

Enamels had already been used on pottery, glass and metal and they were soon adapted for use on porcelain with a wide range of colour. Recognition of typical colouring and brush-work is a major aid to identification, as so many fine pieces remained unmarked, and so many marks belonging to wares which were selling well were pirated that to rely on factory marks is impossible. Only if there are other indications that the porcelain is of a specific factory can they be taken as conclusive proof.

It was during the Baroque period that European porcelain was first made, in a style that was exuberantly decorative and which, in the seventeenth century, superseded the classicism of the Renaissance. About 1730 a new form emerged, the Rococo, which originated in France. It consisted of a swirling asymmetrical use of opposing curves, scrollwork, and leaping flourishes. At its best it was the pinnacle of sophisticated elegance, at its worst it descended into vulgarity. About 1760 the inevitable swing in taste, which can be observed throughout history, brought back classicism to popularity, interest being heightened by the archaeological discoveries made at Herculaneum. The Neo-classical period extended into the early nineteenth century, while Napoleon's campaign in Egypt introduced sphinxes and griffons as decorative motifs. Today the porcelain collector has the twofold problem of identification and restoration in the search for rare and beautiful pieces.

# CHINA

## Han and the Six Dynasties

A porcellaneous body was first used as early as the Han dynasty (206 BC–AD 220). The body is a grey stoneware, over which a slip of warm or whitish colour is washed. The glaze is feldspathic and was described by the Chinese by the word tzu, a term which refers to the material's resonance rather than its translucency which is not apparent in the thick early wares. In the West it has been termed proto-porcelain. In form the early wares show the influence of metal vessels, the glazes coming close to the colours of patinated bronze; greens and browns predominate and decoration is incised or combed. Relief modelling was also adapted from bronze prototypes. The Han period was followed by the Six Dynasties during which kaolin and chinastone were discovered; this, when fired, produced a white body.

(*right*) Han jar with lid.
(*below*) Chin celadon ram.

Yüeh celadon pot and three outlined shapes typical of T'ang.

## T'ang (618–906)

A translucent porcelain was first made in the early T'ang period. A fine white body was produced with a thick glaze which ran like treacle, gathering where it stopped, well clear of the base, into 'teardrops'. Celadon ware, which has a greyish-green semi-opaque glaze over a grey body, belongs mainly to the period of the Five Dynasties (907–59) and the Sung, but it is first mentioned in the eighth century. The celadons of Yüeh vary in shade from the colour of putty, through grey-greens to jade; decoration of fish and floral motives are incised or carved into the body. The wares of the period were frequently stacked in the kiln on a bed of sand which can sometimes be found adhering to the bases. The greyish proto-porcelain was still made, with glazes of green, brown and black. A typical T'ang shape is full and globular, the neck narrow, flaring out to a wide flange. Some forms of the T'ang period, such as amphoras and pilgrim bottles, display the influence of Greek and Western culture which reached China both directly and via Persia. Elaborate ewers closely imitating metal forms, conical tea bowls, both deep and shallow bowls, vases with egg-shaped body, and dishes of various kinds were made and also figures and models of animals.

7

## Sung (960–1279)

The Sung period saw the production of the finest Chinese ceramics. Porcelain depended at this time almost entirely on beauty of line and colour and, in an age of refined aesthetic appreciation, it was collected and received royal patronage for the first time. Nevertheless the dates and origins of the wares were most inadequately recorded. Kilns whose wares were regarded as classical were the Ch'ai, the Ju, the Kuan, the Ting and the Ko, the earliest being the Ch'ai which produced a blue porcelain described in the records as 'blue as the sky after rain, seen through the rifts in the clouds'. Ju was a porcellaneous stoneware of a buff colour, with a smooth opaque glaze in greenish-blue and lavender which crazed into fine or coarse crackle. The Kuan body was of a darker hue, showing at the rim and the base through the glaze as a 'brown mouth and iron foot'. The glaze was smooth and semi-opaque, in turquoise, grey, green and blue. Ting was a translucent porcelain of a fine ivory white, the paste showing a warm colour when held to the light; it was decorated with incised and moulded designs. A practice of firing bowls mouth downwards necessitated leaving the rims unglazed, which explains why they were sometimes bound with a silver or copper band.

Many wares are mentioned in Chinese literature which have

(*left*) Ko crackled glazed bowl.
(*below*) Ju bowl on petal stand.

(*above*) Sung thick-glaze bowl.
(*right*) Lung-ch'üan celadon vase.

yet to be identified. Ting ware with a yellowish glaze is known but red and purple are also spoken of. Ko was a stoneware with a dark body covered by a greyish-white glaze, the fine crazing of which was enhanced by a dark pigment. Among the many fine porcelains produced during this period were the Tz'u-chou wares, with a grey body which was coated with a white slip and then decorated by incising through to the darker ground, or with brushwork using slip of another colour. Lung-ch'üan made fine celadons the body of which, where it was left uncovered by glaze, burned to a dark brown. Chien-yao was a highly fired stoneware whose rich dark glaze flowed thickly down to congeal in a roll or a series of 'teardrops', short of the base. It was splashed and streaked black and brown with silver markings, sometimes so delicately as to be aptly called 'Hare's foot fur'.

Decoration with a brush first appeared in the Sung period and foot rims tended to take the place of flat bases. Typical shapes of the period are the two handled 'mallet' celadons, some low bellied vases tapering gracefully to a thin neck band, and high-shouldered vases gently narrowing to a neck surmounted by a wide flange; all clear, graceful shapes.

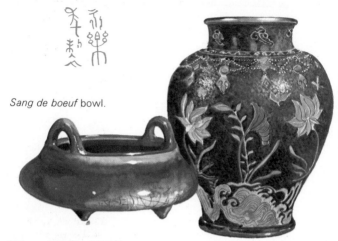

Cloisonné type decorated vase.

Sang de boeuf bowl.

## Ming (1368–1644)

In 1369, in the reign of Hung-wu (1368–98), an Imperial porcelain factory was started in the town of Ching-tê chên which became the most important ceramic centre in China. Reign marks were used for the first time, but as identical marks were added in the K'ang-hsi period to pieces made in homage to the earlier wares, they are more misleading than helpful. Much fine plain white porcelain was made and the reign of Yung-lo (1403–24) saw the making of finely potted eggshell-thin bowls of great delicacy. Early in the Ming period a technique was developed for applying coloured glazes at a reasonably low temperature direct to the body. Outlines of the design were done in raised slip or were incised before the first firing. Both oil and leaf gilding were used. For use in underglaze painting a fine cobalt blue was imported from western Asia and whole new fields of decoration were opened up to the artists by such new materials put at their disposal. Birds, animals, flowers, plants and figures were drawn on to the biscuit body with a calligraphic flow of line. In the reign of Hsüan-tê (1426–35), an underglaze copper red known as 'Sacrificial Red' was also produced, used usually with a simple motif such as three apples, or two fishes.

10

## Middle Ming

By the middle of the Ming period the beauty of the accidental, which had played so great a part in early Chinese wares, was replaced by a deliberate smoothness of finish, fine decoration and brilliance of colour. A division of labour developed in the production process with the potter finishing his work and turning it over to the decorator. Favoured colours were green, yellow, aubergine, turquoise and dark blue and three-colour and four-colour ware was made. Motifs for designs were drawn from Confucian, Taoist and Buddhist subjects and emblems, and symbols such as the Eight Precious Things, the Dragon of Happiness and Longevity, the Three Rams of Spring etc. By the reign of Ch'êng-hua the early sources of the fine blue underglaze cobalt had run out; in the reign of Hung-chih (1488–1505), a fine yellow was produced, used in coloured grounds and glazes to great effect and described as 'Yellow of the Sunflower' and in a paler version as 'Steamed Chestnuts'. Dating from the Chêng-tê period, 1506–21, which also produced some notable yellow wares with incised green dragons, is some particularly fine blue-and-white which suggests new supplies of cobalt from Persia. The reign of Chia-ching, 1522–66, is marked by the end of the use of 'Sacrificial Red', the supply having been exhausted. It was replaced by an iron-red over-glaze which tends to be iridescent.

治大
年明
製弘

Chêng-tê wig stand.

## Late Ming

With the reign of Wan-li, 1573–1619, the great period of Ming ends. A great deal of blue-and-white was made for export (the blue having a violet shade) and pierced decoration was often used; the style and technical development of porcelain were influenced by the manufacture founded in Ching-tê chên by Hung-wu, first Ming emperor, to serve the court at Nanking. At the court the fashion was for huge fish-bowls which were extremely difficult to make. At Tê-hua a fine white porcelain, known as *Blanc de Chine*, was used, from which figures, sometimes with detachable heads and hands, were made. The Kuan-yin, a female deity, is somewhat reminiscent of a Christian Virgin and Child as she sometimes holds a baby in her arms; Kuan-ti, the god of war, Darhuma and other deities and sages were also subjects for models. The earlier figures are milk-white; a chalky colour is generally thought to indicate a later date. Probably Swatow ware, decorated in a free and lively way with maritime subjects in underglaze blue, and red and green overglaze, was also produced at Tê-Hua.

*Blanc de Chine* figure of a sage.

泰昌

## Ch'ing dynasty or Manchu (1644–1912)
### K'ang-hsi (1662–1722)

The town of Ching-tê chên having been in decline for some time and eventually burnt to the ground, the Manchu Emperor K'ang-hsi rebuilt it and by the end of his reign 3000 kilns were at work. By good fortune a Jesuit missionary, Père d'Entrecolles, took a keen interest in ceramics and wrote detailed accounts in his letters from Ch'ing of the activities of the potteries. Division of labour became geared to mass production, as many as seven workers doing their specialised job on one piece; this output was mainly for the vastly increasing export market and was highly decorated in the European taste.

A great deal of blue-and-white ware was made and improved techniques of purifying materials produced the whitest body and clearest sapphire blue in the underglaze decoration known as Nanking ware. Best known in Europe is the porcelain made mainly for export, listed under the headings of *famille verte*, *famille jaune*, *famille noire* and *famille rose*, the green being the earliest. The *rose*, which was a European innovation, is mostly attributed to the next reign. *Sang de boeuf*, a rich blood-red streaked glaze, is an important ware of the K'ang-hsi period.

(*right*) K'ang-hsi *famille noire* vase.
(*below*) Ch'ing soft-paste hare.

## Yung-chêng (1723–35)

The period is renowned for its refined elegance, but it is most famed for its development of the rose enamel giving its name to the *famille rose* wares. This is a purplish pink produced by using an enamel on a gold chloride base, a method which originated in Europe. It was used sometimes as a monochrome. Dishes having the colour on the back are known as 'ruby-backed'. The *famille rose* ware is not to be confused with the over-ornate Canton ware produced for the export market in vast quantities, especially in the nineteenth century, which has pink as a predominating colour. Increasing interest was taken by the Chinese in the wares of the fine early periods, and skilful copies were made, especially by a potter named T'ang Ying who reproduced T'ang, Sung and Ming porcelain. The correct Yung-chêng reign mark was usually used but this was frequently ground out at a later date. Western styles were a great influence on contemporary pieces and paintings of landscapes and figure groups were done in which the Chinese adaptation of the European scene has a charm of its own. 'Rice-grain' decoration, copied from the Persian Gombroon ware, was used during the period; it was made by piercing the body before firing with small holes in the shape and size of rice-grains, and allowing the glaze to fill them when fired.

Yung-chêng *famille rose* plate.

14

(*above*) Chi'en Lung armorial
plate.
(*right*) Jesuit bowl.

## Ch'ien Lung (1736–95)

This period is regarded as one of decline. Technique was beyond reproach but ran ahead of aesthetic considerations, as in the imitations of wood, jade and even rhinoceros horn! A strange aberration was the lacquering of the body with black, into which were set pieces of mother-of-pearl. Flambé ware was popular, and large vases were made with a flaming red glaze streaked with violet and purple. A charming export porcelain was the Jesuit ware on which religious subjects were painted after engravings, in fine black lines, with an added touch of gold. A Chinese interpretation of an angel is especially appealing. Orders were taken at Canton for the painting of armorial bearings, mainly on tableware. This porcelain was thought, rather oddly, to have been produced at Lowestoft in England at one time and is still known in the trade as Chinese Lowestoft. Snuff bottles are largely ascribable to late Ming and the nineteenth century.

# The nineteenth century in China

The prosperous years of Ch'ien Lung were followed by years of unrest, rebellion, and foreign intervention. Imperial patronage was replaced by direction from provincial authorities. In the middle of the century Ching-tê-chên was razed to the ground during the Taiping rebellion and rebuilt in 1864. During the reign of Chia-ch'ing (1796–1821, not to be confused with an earlier Chia-ch'ing of the sixteenth century), earlier styles of porcelain were repeated with a high standard of craftsmanship. Typical of the period is a large variety of snuff bottles, glazed and in biscuit, carved or finely enamelled, and miniature bottles in a range of colours from the speckled 'robin's egg' to more usual greens and yellows. By the reign of Tao Kuang (1821–50) the porcelain was of an inferior quality. Wares were potted more thinly, the body was of a chalky white and the 'muslin' surface of the glaze more pronounced. Overglaze colours combined the palette of the *famille rose* and the *famille verte* but were dominated by an increasing use of iron-red, perhaps because this colour is an obliging one to handle. Typical of this period, apart from the usual reproductions of earlier pieces, are covered bowls, sometimes engraved as well as painted, with decorations in reserves left in a ground colour. The pierced 'rice-grain' pattern was used and a great deal of inferior blue-and-white ware was also made.

Part of Canton bowl showing
detail of pattern.

大清道
光年製

Inlaid Korean celadon vase.

# KOREA

Wares of a porcellaneous nature, a vitrified stoneware, were made in Korea from an early period. The Silla (BC 57–AD 936) corresponds to the Chinese Han, Six Dynasties and Tang; the Koryu (936–1392), during which fine celadons were made, corresponds to the Sung and Yuan. There is a great similarity in the wares of Korea and China and it is frequently a matter of doubt as to which country to ascribe them. Certain forms are typical – the lobed or ribbed boxes and pots and the deep footrims with openwork possibly to enable heating from below. White, cream, black and brown-glazed wares are found in Korea which may be more correctly ascribed to China, but the grey-green and putty coloured celadons inlaid with coloured clays are typical. In various forms, inlay work and painted decoration in black, brown and white slip continued to be used throughout the Yi period, AD 1392–1910. Some Korean wares of the period have a rough strength and beauty, relying a great deal on texture and happy accident to glaze and colour in the kiln.

# JAPAN

## Kakiemon

The secrets of porcelain making are said to have been brought to Japan in the early sixteenth century from Ching-tê chên, the great centre of the ceramic industry of China. It is said that Korean potters brought to work in Japan first discovered porcelain stone in Izumiyama, Arita. The earliest wares were decorated with a pale blue underglaze but by the middle of the seventeenth century overglaze colours were used in the Chinese manner. Two distinct types of ware were made, the Kakiemon and the Imari. The Kakiemon was made by the Sakaida family of whom twelve members are recorded as working between the early seventeenth century and the end of the nineteenth century. Originally inspired by the greatly esteemed porcelain of Chinese Ming, Japanese wares gradually developed their own character. The porcelain was of a fine milk white, the surface of which was decorated but not obscured by exquisitely balanced off-centre designs. Dishes, bowls and plates were frequently made in octagonal and fluted forms which concealed the warping, which sometimes occurred in the firing, better than circular wares. Pieces were decorated with birds, animals, figures and flowers. Both the form and painting of the Kakiemon were a great influence on early European porcelain.

Kakiemon plate with flower decoration.

(*left*) Imari cat.
(*below*) Imari brocade pattern bowl.

## Imari

In 1641 the Dutch were given a trade monopoly and brought Arita wares to Europe. Among the pieces they imported were those with decorations inspired by designs from dyeing and weaving. The brocade patterns became very popular with the European market and the Japanese enamellers were encouraged to produce great quantities of the wares, which became known by the name of the port, Imari, from which they were shipped. Japanese taste was more conservative and the highly decorated pieces known as 'Oriental' were made by the factories of the time specifically for export. Most of the finest ceramics produced at the time are undoubtedly still in Japan. The Imari designs were drawn in blackish-blue underglaze; in the overglaze a dark red predominated, and a great deal of gold was used. The success of these Arita wares was so great that the Chinese began to copy them as early as 1700 and they were still being produced in Japan in the nineteenth century.

Nabeshima bowl with comb pattern base.

## Nabeshima Okawachi

At Okawachi, near Arita, porcelain was made under the direction of the House of Nabeshima. Founded by the Prince of Saga at the beginning of the eighteenth century, it produced some of the finest porcelain in Japan, mostly for the royal household. The paste is fine and white, the decoration much in the style of Kakiemon. A great deal of blue-and-white was made and motifs for decoration were taken from the silk fabrics of Yuzen. A precision in the repetition of patterns was achieved by drawing the design on thin tissue with a medium which would transfer easily with pressure on to the biscuit. The lines were then painted over in cobalt underglaze. The overglaze colours subsequently applied obscure this original working in the early wares, but later less carefully painted pieces reveal the underdrawing. A typical motif of Nabeshima ware is a comb design round the base rim of the dish.

Japanese marks are numerous and misleading. It is sufficient to give only a few examples since many potters' marks were granted by patrons, and seals were passed on to their pupils and may appear on work by several generations.

Three typical impressed signatures
(1) Banko (2) Ninsei (3) Dohachi.

# Hirado Mikawachi

A little later than the wares of the Arita factories, the kilns of Mikawachi, started by Korean craftsmen for the production of pottery, also began to manufacture porcelain. From 1751 the kilns were patronised by Prince Matsura of Hirado and subsequently by his successors, the best of the porcelain being reserved for the royal household. The wares were not therefore exported before 1850. Mikawachi wares have a distinct quality which sets them apart from other contemporary porcelain. The pure white paste, made from Amakusa stone, is devoid of any greyness and coldness and pieces were usually small but very fine, decorated mostly in a pale, slightly violet-toned, underglaze blue and sometimes with relief and incised work. Celadon ware was also made and models of figures, beasts, birds and fabulous animals, and some extremely delicate sprays of blossom and foliage were produced. Characteristic are slender-necked wares which are of extreme refinement and delicacy. The port of Hirado, from which the wares were exported, gave them the name by which they are best known. Later nineteenth-century Mikawachi porcelain is inferior in quality.

Mikawachi wine cup stand.

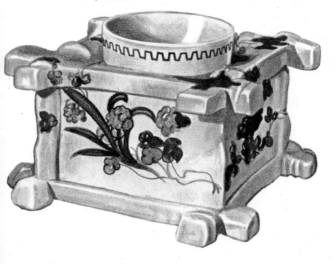

## Kutani

Kutani was a village in the mountains of Kaga province which was to become as important in the east for the production of porcelain as Nabeshima was in the west. The kilns were established in the middle of the seventeenth century by the House of Maeda. The Japanese describe Kakiemon as 'refined and elegant' but Kutani as 'magnificent'. There is a characteristic breadth of design in form and ornament and a boldness in colour, the latter being made necessary originally perhaps by the imperfections of glaze and paste. Rich purple, green and blue-green, yellow and red are typical of the Kutani palette with the details outlined in black. Though some wares were influenced by the late Ming and early Ch'ing of China, much was purely Japanese in inspiration, patterns being adapted from woven fabrics and sometimes used in relief. After a long period of success the factory declined but was revived in the early nineteenth century. The body was no longer white, however, and the overglaze colours lacked their original clarity and richness; also iron-red and gold were more widely used at this time than before.

## Kyoto

At the Kyoto factory the technique of porcelain making was learned from the Arita factories at the beginning of the nineteenth century, and imitations of Chinese wares of the Ming and Ch'ing dynasties, as well as blue-and-white, celadon and three-colour ware, were made.

## Seto

Seto became in the early nineteenth century a great centre for the production of porcelain and immense quantities of blue-and-white ware were made. Seto also made and exported huge and dubiously decorated vases, much admired by the Victorians who used them to hold ostrich feathers, bulrushes and ornamental grasses, and as umbrella stands.

## Satsuma

The Satsuma factory, like most of the Japanese factories, was established by Korean potters and did not produce porcelain till the end of the eighteenth century. At this time a hard white body was made with a characteristic ivory glaze on which decorations were overglazed in the brocade style. In the early pieces enamelling was restrained, setting off the ivory glaze. Later work showed an increasing use of ornament and gold, until the whole surface disappeared beneath a horror of pictures and gilt.

(*left*) Satsuma incense burner.
(*below*) Kyoto fan-shaped plate.

# GERMANY

## Meissen (from 1710)

In 1710 a porcelain factory was founded at Meissen by Augustus the Strong. It was under the direction of an alchemist from Thuringia named Johann Friedrich Böttger, a man who had dreams of finding the Philosopher's Stone and of transmuting base metals into gold. When he came to Saxony Augustus held him prisoner. Fortunately he was put under the supervision of Baron von Tschirnhausen who had already been researching into the equally esteemed secrets of porcelain manufacture. Von Tschirnhausen died in 1708 but Böttger went on to produce a red stoneware resembling the Chinese Yi-Hsing, so hard that it was treated as a semi-precious stone and cut and polished on a jeweller's wheel. It was not long before a suitable clay was found at Aue which produced a warm creamy-white porcelain although initially the glaze was thick and imperfect. The forms of teapots, vases and tankards, which were among the pieces made, derived from silver and metalware. Grotesque and chinoiserie figures were also produced whose style was often derived from ivory carvings.


## Heroldt (from 1719)

In 1719 Böttger died and the factory was put under the direction of Johann Gregor Heroldt, who was a colour chemist and who succeeded in adding brilliance to the Meissen palette. The porcelain was now thin and fine, decorated in the Chinese and Japanese manner. After 1725 designs were enclosed in gold Baroque scrollwork and a method was evolved for laying ground colours in which reserves were left for decoration. Among the enamellers working after 1730 were C. F. Heroldt, who painted harbour scenes and fine monochromes in black and red, and Adam von Löwenfinck who made lively adaptations of Kakiemon. Thus the oriental influence gradually gave way to an evolving European style inspired by contemporary painting and engravings. The crossed-swords mark of Meissen had been applied at first in enamel; then in 1735 cobalt underglaze was first used although it tended to disappear into the unglazed base. The mark was then put on top until the introduction of domed bases enabled the mark to be glazed.

Vase, style of Löwenfink, before 1735.

Small early Meissen pot.

Kaendler figure of Harlequin.

## Kaendler (from 1731)

In 1731 Johann Joachim Kaendler, whose vigour and plasticity of modelling was rivalled only by Bustelli of Nymphenburg, became *Modellmeister*. At first he worked on large pieces for the Japanese Palace built by Augustus, but towards 1740 he was making small figures and groups with subjects drawn from the Italian Comedy, the court, the market place and the street. He made sets of figures of the Seasons, the Continents, the Arts, the Sciences, and the Elements and also subjects taken from mythology. It was Kaendler who was responsible for the original Monkey Band. The early figures were strongly and simply painted, the flesh almost without tint, the dresses in a pure colour or sprigged with flowers; bases were pad-shaped and encrusted with a few flowers. Other modellers working in Kaendler's style were J. F. Eberlein, Peter Reinicke and F. Elias Meyer. Elaborate tableware was also made in the Baroque taste with figures applied to lids and handles, and tureens were modelled in the form of fruits and vegetables, fishes, birds and animals.

## Academic period (1764–74)

About 1750 production was greatly increased as the export market grew. There was a strong influence of French and Dutch painting on decoration and exquisite miniatures were painted on boxes for snuff and patches, etc. When the Seven Years War began in 1756, the greatest period of Meissen was over. In 1764 C. W. Dietrich, the court painter, was made adviser to the factory and under his guidance design became more formal and displayed a classical symmetry which superceded the Baroque and Rococo. The Louis Seize garlands of flowers and ribbons enclosing monograms, and flowers and birds, were still painted on tableware but with less care and in less attractive colours. The mosaic pattern was introduced at this time. Acier, a French modeller, came to Meissen and under his influence the sculptural quality of the figures gave way to a pretty sentimentality. Lacework was developed and made by dipping gauze into porcelain slip, the gauze being burnt away in the firing. White unglazed bisque was popular and its texture, suggestive of marble, rendered it suitable for portrait busts. The decade between 1764 and 1774 is known as the Academic period, sometimes called the 'dot' period because of the dot inserted between the hilts of the Meissen crossed swords. The earlier 'oriental' style still remained in favour.

Examples of Baroque and high Rococo decoration. (The teapot is Höchst.)

Marcolini cup and saucer.

## Later Meissen

In 1774 Count Camillo Marcolini was made director of the
Meissen factory and set about putting it on its feet financially
by prohibiting the import of foreign porcelain, and selling off
outdated and defective pieces. A great deal of elaborate tableware was exported, especially to Russia and Turkey, but it was
a time of war and disruption for Germany and of fierce competition from foreign markets, not least of all from Josiah
Wedgwood of England, whose jasperware and creamware
had become very popular. Figures were made, the use of
bisque lending itself to copies of antique sculptures. Bases
were round, oval or angular, and decorated with a classical
motif such as a raised key pattern. Jüchtzer was *Modellmeister*
and he and Johann Daniel Schöne both worked in bisque. A
great deal of ware for daily use was made, much of which was in
blue and white. Some ornamental pieces were almost entirely
covered in gold with paintings, which were often of detailed
topography, in the reserves. Grisaille was much in favour but
though technical skill was not lacking artistic vision was
generally at a low ebb. Marcolini died in 1814.

(*right*) Late Meissen cupid vase.
(*below*) Meissen candlestick.

At the beginning of the nineteenth century Andreas Franz Wegner was modelling busts (including one of Alexander of Russia, and of Napoleon) and Schöne copied Wedgwood's jasperware, but there were no new developments of note except perhaps the lithophanes produced about 1828. These were tablets of very thin porcelain on which was impressed a scene. Held up to the light these pictures appear to be three dimensional. From about 1820 to 1840 is known as the Biedermeier period which was the equivalent of English Regency and French Empire (though later in date). By mid-century, with Ernst August Leuteritz as *Modellmeister*, replicas of eighteenth-century models were being made in great quantities but in colours which, however, had a predominance of sentimental blues, pinks and greens, very different from the originals. To the nineteenth century belong the ballerinas with lacy skirts, the flower-encrusted candelabra, mirror frames surrounded by flowers and putti, and elaborate pierced comports. Transfer printing was first used at Meissen in the nineteenth century, although it had been used elsewhere on porcelain, particularly in England, in the eighteenth century.

29

## Höchst (1750–94)

At Höchst a faience factory had been established by Löwenfinck of Meissen. It was here, in 1750, that Johann Benckgraff and J. J. Ringler succeeded in making porcelain. Löwenfinck had been granted a fifty year monopoly by the Elector of Mainz but did not stay to see the porcelain in production. Made from a creamy-white paste, it followed, in form and decoration, the pattern set by Meissen. Lilac or purple monochrome paintings of landscapes and pastoral scenes were executed and the colour, used with gold, also occurred frequently on borders and bases. Most typical of the factory was the highly fanciful polychrome scrollwork surrounding designs of flowers, fruit and birds. Simon Feilner was modeller for a time and to him are ascribed some strong lively figures from the Italian Comedy and genre subjects. Chief modeller in 1767 was Johann Peter Melchior. His groups are pretty and sentimental, the clothes highly decorated, striped and flower-sprigged and painted in soft sugary colours with the pinks predominating. The bases are often of rock formations.

(*above*) Small Höchst figure, c. 1775.
(*below*) Figure of a musician, c. 1775.

Wegely figure, c. 1755.

## Berlin: Wegely's factory (1752–57)

In 1752, with the help and encouragement of Frederick the Great, the Berlin factory was started by Wilhelm Kaspar Wegely, a wool merchant. He was assisted by Johann Benckgraff who was still presumably working at Höchst at the time of the founding of the Berlin factory. The porcelain was fine but extremely highly fired which gave some difficulty with the overglaze colours; much of the work was therefore left white. Chief modeller was Ernst Heinrich Reichard who made genre groups of some originality but much was copied from Meissen, including the Little Cupids in Disguise and figures from the Italian Comedy. Tableware and decorative vases were also made in the prevailing styles of the period.

Frederick was not impressed with the products of the factory and it was closed in 1757.

Berlin allegorical figure group, c. 1770.

## Gotzkowsky and Royal Berlin (from 1761)

In 1756 Meissen was overrun by the Prussian army. In conse-
quence workers from the Meissen factory migrated to Berlin
where a new factory was started by Johann Ernst Gotzkowsky
with Reichard as Art Director. The factory was bought by
Frederick the Great in 1763 and became Royal Berlin, producing
its finest work up to the death of the King in 1786. Tableware
was produced in the Rococo style and decorated in strong
colours with flowers, birds, and scenes after Watteau, Boucher
and the Dutch masters; the influence of Sèvres and Meissen is
apparent in the coloured grounds, pierced borders and mosaic
pattern. Both attractive and original was the use of *camaieu*
or two-coloured flower painting by such notable painters as
K. W. Böhme, Karl Jacob Christian Klipfel and Balthasar
Bormann. *Modellmeister* was Friedrich Elias Meyer, who, with
his brother Wilhelm Christian Meyer, produced some fine
groups with elongated bodies and small heads. Rococo bases
gave way to square or rounded architectural forms suitable to
mythological and allegorical subjects. In collaboration with
the court sculptor Gottfried Schadow and an architect Hans
Christian Genelli, Reise made some very large table-centres,
one of which was presented to the Duke of Wellington.

# Fürstenberg (from 1753)

In 1753 Karl I of Brunswick established a porcelain factory in the castle of Fürstenberg with the assistance of Johann Benckgraff, who had worked at Vienna and Höchst and had been concerned with the founding of the factory at Berlin. For some time the porcelain was faulty and decoration, including relief work, was used to camouflage the defects in the greyish glaze. Up to 1770 the factory worked under great difficulties but produced some fine tableware, including some with raised Rococo scrolls, in the white paste, enclosing painted scenes. Feilner, the modeller, who also came from Höchst, worked much in the style of Kaendler, his figures being full of character, vigorously modelled, and painted with bold simplicity. The bases are usually flat pads with a flower or two. The figures include the fashionable repertoire of the Italian Comedy and genre pieces, amongst which are groups of miners. In 1770 the factory was taken over by the court and proceeded to flourish. Feilner's style was copied by other modellers; a set of monkey musicians begun by Kaendler was made; portrait reliefs, classical figures and busts were made in bisque. Tableware was finely decorated and Berlin and England's Wedgwood exerted considerable influence.

Fürstenberg figures,
(*left*) Pantaloon, (*right*) A miner.

## Nymphenburg (from 1753)

In 1753 Ringler came to Nymphenburg from Vienna, and under the patronage of Count Sigismund von Haimhausen the manufacture of porcelain was established. From 1754 to 1763 it was highly successful, having the finest *Modellmeister* to work in the medium of porcelain, Franz Anton Bustelli. His figures have a dramatic and rhythmic plasticity. In some groups Rococo arabesques spring from the usually thin flat bases, rising as supports for the figures and forming an integral part of the composition, to terminate in a flourish above. His subjects are drawn widely from the Italian Comedy and genre scenes. He made religious groups, putti, musicians, chinoiseries and small trifles such as cane handles, etc. Bustelli used colour sparingly but with strength and simplicity (sometimes his figures are completely white); for instance, he might colour a skirt with a wash of green and leave the apron as white porcelain, sprigged only with flowers. In more highly decorated pieces pattern is not allowed to break up form. Fine tableware was also made at this period and decorated in the Meissen manner. From 1796 to 1822 Melchior was chief modeller.

(*left*) Bustelli group, c. 1760.
(*right*) Columbine, by Bustelli, c. 1760.

Figure of Thetis by Linck, c. 1765.

## Frankenthal (1755–99)

In 1755 Paul Anton Hannong removed his factory at Strasbourg to Frankenthal. This factory had been closed by the
monopoly granted to Vincennes by the French authorities.
Frankenthal paste is fine, milk-white and semi-opaquely
glazed. The chief modeller was Johann Wilhelm Lanz, whose
still doll-like figures have slightly Rococo bases in gilt and
purple. Attributed to J. F. Lück (1758–1764) are some elaborate
groups in the style of Lanz. Konrad Linck, *Modellmeister* from
1762 to 1766, had a distinctive style; his finely modelled figures
are full of movement and richly ornamented with applied
work. The use of rich greens and applied ornament is common
to both Linck and his successor K. G. Lück but the latter treats
his subjects in a distinctively playful manner. Adam Baurer,
*Modellmeister* around 1777, included children in many of his
groups, and Melchior, succeeding him in 1779, worked on
classical and allegorical pieces mainly in bisque. Early tableware was influenced by Meissen, while 'pheasant eye'
pattern, woodgraining, and motifs from textiles are based on
pieces manufactured at Sèvres.

35

## Ludwigsburg (1758–1824)

The factory was started by Bonifacius Christoph Häckher in 1756, but probably only made faience initially. Charles Eugène, Duke of Württemberg, took it over in 1758 and appointed Ringler as director. The porcelain fell below the fine standards of the other German factories but the material had great plasticity and it was in figure modelling that Ludwigsburg excelled. Art director from 1759 to 1779 was G. F. Riedel, who made sketches, engravings, and models which were used later by other factories. He and the chief modeller, Johann Göz, are probably jointly responsible for many early figures in the Rococo style and influenced by Frankenthal. The repairer J. J. Louis was also a modeller and made some amusing Venetian Fair groups as well as various birds and animals; his work is marked with an L. Bases were flat and squarish or decorated with a Rococo scroll. The work of Johann Christian Wilhelm Beyer, *Modellmeister* from 1764 to 1767, was altogether more ambitious, his figures displaying a greater understanding of anatomy and a fullness of rhythm and movement, though his plinth-like bases are Neo-classical.

Ludwigsburg toy theatre with figures.

Small Ansbach pot with animal spout.

## Ansbach (1758–1860)

From 1758 porcelain was made at Ansbach under the patronage of the Margrave Karl Alexander of Brandenburg, with Johann Friedrich Kaendler, a cousin of the Meissen modeller, in charge of production. Early pieces, before 1770, are extremely rare but of fine quality, though the influence of Höchst in its toys and figures is more apparent than the style of individual modellers. One peculiarity of Ansbach is the outlining of the eyes in red.

J. M. Schölhammer was one of the chief painters and, among others, Kühl and Schreitmüller painted flowers, Büttner and Hütter did animals, while Telorac specialised in fruit and J. Stenglein in landscapes. Finely painted tableware in the style of Meissen and Berlin was made including pear-shaped coffee pots with lips decorated with relief masks. Useful and decorative wares, in delicate designs, were often painted in crimson monochrome with landscapes in panels surrounded by rich gilt lacework in a Rococo style typical of the period.

In 1806 the factory was sold but continued to make porcelain until 1860. It had lost impetus after 1791.

## Kelsterbach (1761–1802)

The factory was established in 1761 by the Landgrave Ludwig VIII of Hesse-Darmstadt, at a former faience factory in Kelsterbach, with the help of C. D. Busch of Meissen. The factory was in existence for a very short time, closing in 1768, though it was reopened again between 1789 and 1792 and between 1799 and 1802. The chief modeller of the early period was Johann Carl Vögelmann, formerly of Ludwigsburg. To Vögelmann are ascribed some rather grotesque putti, and some groups of lively but coarsely modelled figures raised on Rococo bases. Another modeller, and also the chief repairer, at this period was P. A. Seefried, who made some copies of Nymphenburg in the style of Bustelli. Little tableware was made but various pieces include cane handles and Rococo snuff boxes, very finely painted in miniature.

Enamellers include J. H. Eger and G. I. Hess. In 1789 the factory was reopened by J. J. Lay but no work of distinction was produced.

# Ottweiller (1763–97)

Under the patronage of Prince Wilhelm Heinrich of Nassau-Saarbrucken, a factory was started at Ottweiller in 1763, with a Frenchman, Etienne Dominique Pellevé, as director. The paste is not a pure white, and the French influence apparent in the forms is due to the modeller Paul Louis Cyfflé, who was employed there around 1765, along with other French artists. The painter Friedrich Karl Wollfahrt worked at Ottweiller about 1765 and a tureen of this period bears his signature. Little is known of the factory and examples of its work are rare but of very fine quality, especially in the painting. Jugs, decorated with Watteau-type scenes or garlands and featherings of gold, are typical, as are painted nudes set in landscapes and surrounded by Rococo scrolls. Some jugs from the factory, pear-shaped in form and with wavy tops and hinged lids, bear a definite resemblance to products of Sceaux and Marseilles and there is evidence of a strong association with French porcelain throughout the short life of the factory, no doubt due to Cyfflé's influence. Few of the many figures made survive.

Ottweiller coffee pot. One of the rare porcelain pieces of this small eighteenth-century factory, it shows a characteristic scene from mythology.

## Fulda (1765–90)

A factory for the production of porcelain was started at Fulda by the Prince Bishop Heinrich von Bibra in 1765. Faience of the highest quality had been produced at Fulda from 1741 under the supervision of Löwenfinck; the production of porcelain in 1765 began unusually late but in the hands of the arcanist Nikolaus Paul and the painter J. P. Schick, the factory produced an exceptionally fine material which was fashioned by modellers and painters of the highest order. Their works are rare and much sought after. The factory was burnt down in 1767 but was reopened about 1769. The style of Fulda is late Rococo and bears a resemblance to Höchst; the figures are smooth and rounded, graceful and delicately painted, having mound or pad bases, sometimes with grass or a flower, sometimes with a Baroque scroll. Subjects are pastoral or courtly; models of musicians or characters from the Italian Comedy were made.

Fine tableware was also made which was painted in both monochrome and polychrome, in the style of Meissen, using red and brown.

Three Fulda figures, c. 1770.

## Cassel (1766–88)

A factory was founded at Cassel in 1766 which was in the hands of Nikolaus Paul, the arcanist. It produced tablewares which were advertised as 'coloured, or blue and white, reeded or smooth' and 'at low prices'. The paste was poor and nothing of much importance was made, though it produced some figures and busts in hard-paste.

## Gutenbrunn (1767–75)

Under the patronage of the Grand Duke Christian IV of Pfalz-Zweibrucken, a porcelain factory was founded in 1767 by Stahl, an arcanist who may have worked at Sèvres. Some porcelain was made from a local clay and decorated with flower motifs, but a finer porcelain was produced from Passau clay brought from Bavaria, which was painted with flowers, landscapes and harbour scenes.

Gutenbrunn coffee pot, c. 1765.

Würzburg jug with lid, c. 1775.

C · G
W

## Würzburg (1775–80)

Under a privilege from the Prince-Bishop Adam Friedrich, Count of Seivsheim, a factory was founded by Johann Caspar Geyger at Würzburg in 1775. Its duration was brief and not a great deal is known about it. The paste and decoration were in some ways rudimentary, but more ornamental tableware was made, using the decorative motifs of 'mosaic' bands and flowered garlands; a jug with the medallion mark of about 1775 has bands of raised pattern, applied mask lip, and a swirling handle of a fabulous beast. It is decorated by a carefully painted landscape.

Figures have been ascribed to Würzburg but have not been authenticated beyond doubt. They are simple and rather arbitrary copies after Höchst, in a coarse greyish paste with a faulty glaze, and include characters from the Italian Comedy.

# Thuringia

A number of factories were established in Thuringia, owing to the presence of a suitable clay and a plentiful supply of fuel from the forests. The enterprises were mostly private ones and more concerned with commerce than aesthetics. Out of the following factories, the Greiner family owned seven.

## Kloster-Veilsdorf (1760)

At this Thuringian factory a fine milk-white porcelain was produced, some of which was finely decorated by an unidentified artist with naturalistic flowers, scenes with figures and landscapes with classical ruins. Figures were also made, those from the Italian Comedy with mound bases, and classical figures having sprigged robes on square bases. The Prince died in 1795 and the factory eventually came under the control of the Greiner family.

## Gotha (1757)

At the Gotha works a similar type of porcelain was made. The factory was founded by Wilhelm von Rotberg and it is thought that Nikolaus Paul had some connection with it. In 1772 Rotberg leased the factory to three of his workers, Johann Adam Brehm, Johann Georg Gabel and Christian Schulz, and they produced some fine wares in the Louis Seize and Neo-classical styles: figures, tableware, vases and medallions as well as figurines and portrait busts in biscuit. Decoration was carried out in black and brownish red monochrome.

Kloster-Veilsdorf bowl, c. 1770.

### Volkstedt

This was established in 1760 for the making of soft-paste porcelain. Imitations of Meissen were made (including the mark) and other work was carried out in the Meissen style. Some large vases were produced with decoration of flowers, fruit and figures in landscape, and with Rococo scrollwork under the motif.

### Wallendorf

Wallendorf was founded by Hammann in 1764. Chiefly blue and white tableware. Cups and bowls with ribbed surfaces are typical wares.

### Limbach

Founded by Gotthelf Greiner himself in 1772. Mainly figures, very unsophisticated, but pleasing. Some have bases with a characteristic painted scroll, others have simple pads.

### Ilmenau

Founded in 1764 by Christian Grabner. Specialised in small plaques imitating Wedgwood's jasperware.

Coffee pot decorated at Augsburg.

### Gera
Founded by Johann Gottlob Ehwald, and mostly known for decoration imitating the grain of wood.

### Grosbreitenbach
Anton von Hopfgarten was the founder. Tablewares were made, most frequently decorated with landscapes. Other less important factories belonging to the Greiner family were at Ravenstein, Katzhutte, Tettau and Schney.

## Hausmaler
*Hausmaler* were independent enamellers who used undecorated porcelain, mainly from Meissen and Vienna, sold off by the factories when it became outmoded. Decoration is therefore frequently later than the paste. Early *Hausmaler* used unfired impermanent colours and fell into disrepute, but much of their later, fired work, was so fine that the factories gave out work to them. At times *Hausmaler* became too competitive with the factories, who stopped sales of white wares to them. In France the outside decorator was known as a *chambrelan* while in England James Giles was a 'China and enamel painter'.

45

# VIENNA (1719–1864)

In 1718 the Holy Roman Emperor, Charles VI, granted to Claudius Innocentius du Paquier a monopoly for the production of porcelain. In 1719 the factory was in production, but suffered a setback when his kilnmaster Stölzel returned to Meissen in 1720, taking with him the enameller J. G. Heroldt. Hunger also left to go to Stockholm and, eventually, to St Petersburg.

The porcelain has a greenish tinge and its form is derived from silver and metalware. Applied masks, acanthus leaves, fabulous animals and figures decorate spouts, lids and handles. Rich but formal pattern often covers the ground, Baroque scrolls enclose diaper patterns, trellises, formalised fruit baskets, trees, birds, chinoiseries and scenes with figures. As well as brilliant gem-like colour, monochrome was used, and gold and silver were applied lavishly. Single figures are rare.

(*above*) Du Paquier tureen.

(*below*) Du Paquier double-handled cup and five typical cup shapes.

46

Du Paquier lady with a fan.

In 1744 the factory became insolvent and was bought by the Austrian State. From this time on the shield mark was used. Decoration in the Rococo style was similar to Meissen, but typical of Vienna are the shell, leaf, and osier patterns in relief on tableware, and an attractive monochromatic scheme in green and black. Later on the influence of Sèvres is shown in the use of rich blue grounds overlaced with gold. Models include grotesques and figures from the Italian Comedy, and Leopold Dannhauser made crinoline figures some without bases. The work of Johann Joseph Niedermeyer is best known; his small-headed doll-like figures are painted in pale clear colours. The bases of this period were either high and scrolled, or small and decorated with painted scrolls or formal patterns. From 1784 to 1805 the factory was directed by Sorgenthal; fine highly decorated tableware was made, the ground entirely covered by gold, with tooling and exquisite miniature painting. In the nineteenth century the factory copied its early work and earlier unpainted porcelain was frequently decorated.

Medici double-necked bottle, c. 1560.

## ITALY

### Florence: Medici (1575–87)

In 1575 the first soft-paste porcelain to be made in Europe was manufactured at the Medici factory founded by the Grand Duke Francesco I. Ever since Marco Polo had returned home in 1295 bringing back examples of oriental porcelain, attempts had been made to copy it. The nearest that had been achieved was an imitation of the material in opaque white glass. With the help of a potter, said to have been a Levantine, a rather imperfect vitreous body with a thick bubbly glaze was made at the Medici kilns, which were in the Boboli Gardens. The wares show in form and decoration an influence of Florentine maiolica, of Chinese porcelain of the sixteenth century and of Turkish and Persian pottery. A great variety of shapes and forms were made: spouted and lipped jugs, double bottles for oil and vinegar, flasks, bowls, plates, dishes and vases. Pieces were elaborated with moulded forms of masks and leaves applied to the body; painted decoration was mostly done in underglaze cobalt blue, but on some pieces yellow and copper-green were applied. The factory closed at the death of its founder in 1587 but some work seems to be of a later date.

# Venice: Vezzi (c. 1720–27)

The Venetian factory was founded by Francesco Vezzi; a goldsmith and a man of business, it is probable that he met Christopher Konrad Hunger during his travels to Vienna. Hunger, a specialist in underglaze painting and overglaze enamelling, had betrayed the secrets of Meissen to the factory at Vienna and now came to Venice to assist in the establishment of the Vezzi factory. During its short life it made fine hard-paste porcelain but was closed after only seven years due to a financial crisis and the kilns were destroyed. The colour of the body varied a great deal from a good white to a grey or sometimes yellowish tone but it was always very translucent. Kaolin from Germany was used when it could be got but its export was prohibited and the difficulty of procuring it illicitly may be responsible for the variation in quality. The glaze was transparent and glassy, sometimes made less so by a haze of small bubbles. Designs were adopted from metalwork of the period with much application of decorations in moulded relief. The finest work of Vezzi compares favourably with that of Meissen and Vienna and, like those factories, it found its decorative inspiration in Kakiemon and the exotic wares of China; however, the majority of pieces tend to be less sophisticated and to be more naïvely and broadly painted.

Vezzi gondola lantern, c. 1725.

Hewelcke portrait plaque, c. 1763.

## Nathaniel Hewelcke (1756–63)

In 1728 the Venetian Board of Trade, in an effort to encourage the development of local potteries, offered as an incentive aid and facilities to anyone who would set up kilns for the production of fine porcelain and maiolica. It was not until 1758 that Nathaniel Hewelcke and his wife Dorothea applied for, and were granted, a monopoly for the production of porcelain for twenty years. These two were refugees from Meissen, where the potteries had been disrupted by the outbreak of the Seven Years War, Dresden having been occupied by Frederick the Great of Prussia. The factory produced a body of hard-paste, which was not very fine and frequently faulty, the glaze on which was rather dull. Domestic pieces, plaques and groups of animals and birds were made but much of the painting was undistinguished, giving the pieces a rather provincial air.

## Le Nove (1762–1825)

Giovanni Antonibon was the owner of a factory for the manufacture of *terraglie fine* (maiolica), which he had started in 1728. In 1752 he began to experiment in the making of porcelain but did not succeed until 1762. There is some difference of opinion as to whether the body he produced should be regarded as soft- or hard-paste. It is greyish in tone and is covered by a glassy glaze which, where it has run thick, has a brownish tone. Forms were derived from silver and metalware of the period and much of the decoration was influenced by that done on the *terraglie fine*. Plates were decorated with mythological scenes and ornamental pieces had landscapes painted within raised scrollwork; cupids, foliage and shells etc. were applied in full relief to vases. In 1781 ill health caused Antonibon to close his factory from time to time and in 1781 he leased it to Francesco Parolin.

Antonibon vase, c. 1765.

Nove
*

51

Francesco Parolin was to run the factory successfully for twenty years. He had as chief modeller Domenico Bosello, who made figure groups from the Commedia dell'Arte, genre pieces, musicians, dancers, children and putti etc., usually with Rococo bases. The enameller was an eccentric named Giovanni Marcon who was reputed only to have worked on Tuesdays! A fine painter, he developed the use of contrasting tones of the same colour, and also added to the colours of the Nove palette. Designs were adapted from Italian engravings done by the Remondini press and chinoiseries, landscapes, harbour scenes, classical subjects and, after the defeat of the Austrians by Napoleon, commemorative battle scenes, were all used as subjects for decoration. Both in form and enamelling much of the ware was close to that of the Cozzi factory which was in operation at the same time. Many pieces made at the end of the century show the influence of Sèvres and the predomination of the classical style, but all the Italian factories show a strong national character from the earliest times. In 1802 the factory passed from the hands of Parolin to those of Giovanni Baroni.

Parolin vase, c. 1800.

Nove

G. B.      MGS
            B

Baroni urn-shaped vase, c. 1810.

Giovanni Baroni became director of the factory at a time when the Neo-classical style was well under way. Large urn-shaped vases were popular, on which were painted scenes from mythology and the classics, battle scenes and military groups which included oriental figures. Some charming domestic pieces were produced, among which were cups and saucers with a *trompe l'oeil* motif of a military print peeling up at the edges. Bosello the modeller was still working for Le Nove in 1810, and made some groups in plain white, an uncoloured state being popular with all European factories at that time. Baroni was director until 1825, since when the Le Nove factory has remained a flourishing centre of ceramics production to the present day. The factory mark was a painted star.

## Cozzi (1764–1812)

In 1764 Geminiano Cozzi founded a porcelain factory at San Giobbe, aided by workmen from Le Nove, including Pietro Lorenzi, who helped Antonibon establish that factory. The pastes of both factories were similar – greyish, with a wet-looking glaze. Early forms, the body of which was more thickly potted than German wares, were Rococo and elaborate, with applied leaves, flowers and masks. Pear-shaped jugs were made with spouts, which typically had top lips which swept upwards, and handles of leaf forms. Latticework dishes, painted with garlands of flowers, were made in the 1770s, as well as some charming cups, enamelled in a basketwork design. Monochromes were done in greyish blue with touches of flesh-colour, while coats of arms were painted against a background of landscapes filled with figures and classical ruins. Decoration was done in gold alone, and sometimes a delicate tracery of goldwork was superimposed on a ground of soft iron-red. Colour was good and incisive; mauve, red, yellow, blue, blue-green and a fine emerald were used. One of the painters was Lodovici Ortolani, formerly at Le Nove. Cozzi, backed by the Venetian senate, developed a thriving export business, which continued through the Napoleonic invasion and ended in 1812.

Ginori coffee pot, c. 1775.

## Doccia (1735 to the present)

The best authenticated Italian factory is that founded by the
Marchese Carlo Ginori in 1735 under a sanction obtained from
the Grand Duke of Tuscany, Francisco III. The factory was
established on the old site of the Medici kilns at Doccia, near
Florence. The porcelain paste known as *masso bastardo,* was
extremely grey in colouring, for which reason, perhaps, after
1770 tin oxide was added to the glaze which gave it a white
opacity. The earlier wares have a green tinge to the glaze, very
noticeable in some white cups and saucers, with a raised pattern
in the Chinese style. As chemists Ginori employed Giovanni
Targioni-Tozzètti and Jean Baillou: Johann Carl Wendelin
Anbreiter von Zirnfeld, a painter formerly at du Paquier's
factory at Vienna, came to work at Doccia bringing with him
some technical knowledge as well as his skill. Chief modeller
was Gaspare Bruschi; designs in wax by a noted sculptor,
Massimiliano Soldani-Benzi, were the base for porcelain groups.

A variety of domestic wares were made such as tall coffee pots with snake-like handles, long upright spouts joined to the neck by a decorative bar, and domed lids (which became flatter at a later date). Teapots with swan-necked spouts, also at times joined by a scroll to the main body, tall cups without handles, dishes fluted or with wavy edges, enriched by moulded scrolls and shells, and covered bowls were among the objects produced. Some pieces were double walled, made in imitation of the Tê-hua wares of China with the outer shell of openwork tracery. Painted pieces were decorated with religious subjects, figures from contemporary life, subjects from mythology, flowers, plants, richly embellished coats of arms and birds in landscapes. The painting was often extremely finely done and frequently has the fine-haired brush strokes and stippling of a miniaturist. The colour was striking with mauves and violets against iron-red, yellow and a clear bright emerald green. Vienna exerted an influence on both form and decoration, as did famous pieces of sculpture like the Laocoön which were copied directly. Contemporary Italian paintings and bronzes also provided the models for large relief plaques.

Doccia floral plate, c. 1760.

Lorenzo Ginori (1757–1791) greatly increased production when he took over the directorship on the death of his father, Carlo Ginori. A glaze containing tin oxide was introduced and the paste itself, which had been liable to firecracks, was improved. New forms were introduced, such as tureens with entwined handles, decorated with applied flowers on the lid, bowl and stand, or knobs modelled in fruit, vegetable and flower forms. Forms in general became lighter and cups began to have handles. Decoration in relief was used and much of this ware was made from old Capodimonte moulds. Decoration was sometimes done in the Imari style and chinoiseries were painted in gold. Finely detailed work was done in pure monochrome as well as polychrome, using a variety of subject matter – for example, harbour scenes, markets, figure groups of Europeans and Turks, fighting cocks in red and gold, European flowers, and a tulip motif derived from Persia or Turkey. Ground colours show the influence of Sèvres; then latterly a more translucent paste was used which was a finer white. Religious groups and figures of street musicians and so forth were produced.

Lorenzo Ginori figure, c. 1770.

## Capodimonte (1743–59)

The factory at Capodimonte, on the outskirts of Naples, was founded in 1743 by Charles III of Bourbon. His wife, Maria Amalia Christina of Saxony, grand-daughter of Augustus the Strong, brought with her dowry quantities of porcelain from the Meissen factory. A soft-paste was eventually made under the guidance of Gaetano Schepers. The body varied a great deal in colour from cream to lemon and a reddish brown shade. The surface, often good and smooth, sometimes became pimpled and pitted, a fault which accounts for the overglaze at times not being well wedded to the glaze. In charge of enamelling, until his death in 1752, was Giovanni Ceselli; he was followed by Johann Sigismund Fischer from Saxony who died in 1758.

Maria Ceselli specialised in flower painting; Giuseppe della Torre painted a range of subjects from battle scenes to putti. The fine stippling which he used for his realistic technique lent itself to a soft blending of colours. Pale iron-red and mauve in the cloud formations is characteristic of his work.

Capodimonte figure group, c. 1750.

E STE
G

## Naples (1771–1806)

Twelve years after the dismantling of the Capodimonte factory
a new venture was started at Portici, under the patronage of
the son of Charles III, Ferdinand IV of Naples. In 1773 the
factory was removed to new premises built to house it next to
the Royal Palace in Naples. The arcanist was Gaetano Tucci;
Antonio Cioffi and Saverio Maria Grue were enamellers, and
chief modeller was Francesco Celebrano. The factory, not
conspicuous for its originality at first, came into its own with
the advent of the Neo-classical style subsequent to the unearth-
ing of the treasures of Pompeii and Herculaneum. Many
prestige pieces were made, such as elaborate table-services and
centre pieces created as royal gifts. One such service was sent
by Ferdinand to his father in Spain, accompanied by the artists
responsible for the work, bearing a book containing the originals from which the decorations had been adapted. The gift, it
is said, was not graciously received! George III of England
received an equally impressive gift known as the Etruscan
service, part of which is to be seen at Windsor Castle.

Many less pretentious and more attractive pieces were made, in the nature of charming sets of plates with family groups painted over· the centre and indented rims decorated with scrolls and diaper pattern. In 1779 Domenico Venuti was put in charge and under his guidance the best work was produced. Some very typical ware had smaller circular or oval panels painted with scenes of romantic landscape, peasantry, town-scapes and classical ruins, bordered with a gold line sometimes embellished with a pattern. The inside of the plate rim had another gold band and the outer edge was circled by a further band of gold with a classical motif. Painting as a rule was detailed and rather stiff; accurate representations of antique vases were used as decoration and antique vases themselves were reproduced in porcelain.

Some delightful figure modelling was done; groups of strolling figures dressed in the fashion of the time are especially appealing. Portrait busts on plinths were modelled, sometimes in bisque and executed on a large scale.

# Este (1781–95)

The first attempts at the manufacture of porcelain at Este were made in 1765 by G. B. Brunello, formerly a workman at Le Nove, but his efforts were unsuccessful. Jean-Pierre Varion, a modeller of French origin, who had worked at Vincennes and Le Nove, was also with Brunello for a time. About 1778 he went into partnership with a goldsmith and modeller, Gerolamo Franchini, with whom he created an elaborate centre-piece. The top was supported by garlanded putti and decorated with figures, emblems and a winged horse, surrounding a crowning tree. In 1780 Varion died and a year later real production started when, with Varion's pastes and moulds, his widow Fiorina Fabus and her partner Antonio Costa ran the business. The style was Rococo, the pieces almost entirely figures of outstanding quality.

Franchini also established a factory at Este and produced some fine religious figures as well as secular pieces of subjects like the Madrigal and the Comedian. Este figures are essentially sculptural in conception.

Naples, tin-glazed plate, c. 1785.

# FRANCE

## Rouen

The earliest French porcelain was made at Rouen in the late seventeenth century and antedates anything from the German factories; it was however a soft-paste porcelain, the secrets of hard-paste manufacture not being discovered till the middle of the eighteenth century. A patent which included the manufacture of porcelain was granted to Louis Poterat, a faience maker, as early as 1673, but little seems to have been actually produced. Pieces which have been authenticated as Rouen have a decoration in the style of the faience ware with Lambrequins and gadroons painted in fine brushwork in dark blue. Relief work was also used on the body, and in Rouen museum there are some polychrome pieces claimed to be from the factory. Poterat died in 1696.

Early Rouen pot, late seventeenth century.

St Cloud, (*above*) detail of plate, (*right*) leaf-patterned pot.

## St Cloud (1675–1773)

The exact date of the production of porcelain at St Cloud is uncertain; the earliest known surviving pieces are thought to be about 1700. Established by Pierre Chicanneau, the factory was carried on after his death in 1678 by his widow Berthe Coudray. From 1693 the claim was made that 'Porcelain equal to the Chinese' was being produced; however, although St Cloud bears a resemblance to *Blanc de Chine*, it is in fact not a true porcelain but a variety of soft paste or *pâte tendre*. Much white ware was made in a yellowish ivory colour, the glaze so glassy as to appear wet, almost iridescent but having a fine orange-peel surface. The body was inclined to be thick but well formed and the plain white pieces were frequently decorated by a relief pattern of overlapping scales. The raised prunus pattern was also used. Blue and white decoration followed the style of Rouen and faience wares with a typical Baroque diaper patterning being used.

Soft-paste chinoiserie figure
produced at St Cloud c. 1735.

Polychrome decoration under the influence of Kakiemon was
used with a bold simplicity, black, yellow, green, blue and
iron-red being used. The forms of silverware influenced the
design of many pieces. Gadrooning and reeding were used on
cups, bowls, teapots and jugs, and dragon forms were used
for handles. Teapots were made in the form of birds and
figures, and vases and pots were decorated with applied
flowers, foliage and fruit. *Trembleuse* saucers, with galleries to
hold a cup steady in a shaky hand, and figures, including
grotesques, were among the products of the factory, as were
pastille burners, handles for knives and forks, cane tops and
pots pourris, and boxes mounted in silver in the form of simplified animals. The use of silver mounting on a variety of St
Cloud pieces has helped to give at least their latest possible
date. Later products of the factory are of a smokey hue with a
coarser glaze. When Berthe Coudray died in 1772 the factory
passed into the family of her second husband, Henri-Charles
Trou, who had obtained for the factory the protection of the
Duc d'Orléans. Marks given are those not in doubt; they are
sometimes accompanied by unexplained initials.

# Chantilly (1725–1800)

Under the patronage of Louis-Henri, Prince de Condé, experiments in the making of porcelain were made by Ciquaire Cirou and a factory was established in 1725, letters patent being granted in 1735. The prince was an avid collector of Japanese porcelain, in particular of Kakiemon, the surface quality and decoration of which was copied at Chantilly. The addition of tin oxide produced a smooth opaque, milk-white glaze which enhanced the brilliance of the decoration. Blue, red, brown and yellow were colours predominantly used. Tableware, sometimes in lobate form, was made and, the body of the porcelain being more stable than that of Rouen or St Cloud, flat wares were made without trouble. The factories of Vincennes and Sèvres had been established by this time, and their influence is to be seen in the style of decoration and coloured grounds. Porcelain flowers were made, sometimes mounted on a bronze *bocage*. A sprigged flower motif of pinks or carnations with ears of corn and grasses is typical of the factory and was copied by the English factory at Derby and by several others.

Chantilly
(*left*) Pot with lid,
(*centre*) Knife and fork,
(*right*) Cane handle.

## Mennecy (1735–85)

In a small faience pottery, owned by Louis-François de Neufville de Villeroy, a soft-paste porcelain was manufactured by François Barbin. He did not have letters patent from the king and in 1748 he was refused permission to produce his wares in Paris, this being the privilege of the royal factory of Vincennes, whose rights were so well guarded as to prevent the expansion of any rival porcelain manufacture in France. In 1765 Barbin died and the factory was bought by Joseph Julien and Symphorien Jacques. They had for the last three years been running a factory at Sceaux which continued production until 1772, when it was sold to Richard Glot. By 1773 they had abandoned both factories and started another at Bourg-la-Reine. Early wares of Mennecy were based on those of St Cloud, including the opaque glaze, which does not, however, show the faintly pitted surface. An individual style soon evolved. Tableware, sometimes in fluted forms, was decorated with sprays of flowers in which pink roses predominate. A touch of yellow and blue in the other flowers and a bluish green for the leaves completes the palette.

Bourg-la-Reine mustard pot, c. 1756.

Mennecy coffee pot, c. 1755.

Gilding being confined to the royal factory of Sèvres, wares from Mennecy were banded in a purplish pink or, less often, in blue or yellow. The scarcity of flatware suggests some difficulty in its production which would be due to a tendency for the paste to warp in the kiln. Decorative pieces were made, and figures, some of which were finely modelled, others naïve in treatment. Bases were frequently of rock formation washed over with green and brown. Plain white glazed figures were made, and some in biscuit. Chief modeller was Nicholas François Gauron, employed later at Tournai and subsequently at the English factory at Chelsea. Subjects include dwarfs, figures from the Italian Comedy, children, putti and figures from mythology, and fashionable trinkets.

## Sceaux (1763–94)

In about 1748 an architect named de Bey, the owner of a small and unimportant faience factory at Sceaux, took on a craftsman, Jacques Chapelle. At about the same time de Bey applied for permission to make porcelain, but it was refused. Soft-paste porcelain was, however, secretly made there, although not in large quantities until the factory came under the management of two of Chapelle's craftsmen, Joseph Julien and Symphorien Jacques. They worked it in conjunction with the factory of Mennecy until 1772, when it was taken over by Richard Glot, and the products of the two factories are virtually indistinguishable. In 1775 it gained the patronage of the Duc de Penthièvre. Some fine work was carried out by the later factory in the prevailing fashion of the Louis XVI period with paintings of exotic birds and flowers.

Sceaux teapot.

Early Vincennes spray of flowers.

## Vincennes (Sèvres)

The factory was originally founded with the aid of two workmen who had been dismissed from Chantilly, the brothers
Robert and Gilles Dubois. The brother of the Comptroller
General, Orry de Fulvi, had financed the venture and installed
the brothers in part of the Château de Vincennes. Though
saleable porcelain was produced by 1740, the brothers proved
unreliable and were dismissed in favour of another workman
from Chantilly, François Gravant. In 1745 a company was
formed under the name of Charles Adams with a capital of over
90,000 livres and a privilege from the king for a period of
thirty years. Chief administrator was a civil servant named
Boileau; the royal goldsmith Duplessis and a fine enameller,
Mathieu, were put in charge of modelling and painting; the
chemist was Jean Hellot, director of the Academy of Sciences,
and general director from 1746 was Jean-Baptiste de Machault.
Other important figures in the factory's development were
Jean-Jacques Bachelier, working at the factory from 1748 and
Art Director from 1751, and Hulst, or Hults, adviser on matters
of style. The fleur-de-lis was included in the factory mark.

Early Vincennes group, with ormolu mounting.

Decoration of early Vincennes was essentially simple in comparison with the sumptuous wares produced by the later factory at Sèvres. Inspiration came originally from Meissen but a distinctive French style very soon evolved. Rococo forms and ornament were used; paintings of sprigged flowers and insects and figure groups were combined with gilt scrollwork and raised designs of prunus blossom in the paste. Flesh tints were added to the heads and limbs of figures in monochrome. By 1748 the greater part of the production was of porcelain flowers which were not only used to encrust vases and pots pourri but were mounted with metal stems and leaves and set in decorative vases and flower pots. Madame Pompadour once made a perfumed winter garden of porcelain flowers to surprise and delight the king. About 1749 a dark blue underglaze ground was produced known as *gros bleu* and an overglaze ground of a rich blue, the *bleu de roi*. Some figures were made, generally in white glazed porcelain, and bisque was introduced by Bachelier about 1751.

## Vincennes Royal Factory (1752–56)

In 1752, following the death of Orry de Fulvi, a financial crisis lead to the reforming of the company. Privileges were renewed in the name of Eloi Brichard but the secrets of production were reserved by the king, who subscribed 200,000 livres with the right to a quarter of the profits. The factory became the *Manufacture Royale de Porcelaine* and the mark of the crossed Ls was confirmed. Many new restrictions were made to eliminate competition from other factories. Macquer, a chemist of note, worked with Hellot and new colours were introduced, among them the brilliant *bleu turquin*, used as an overglaze ground. A great variety of colour shades were produced which enabled the painter to model his subjects in depth and facilitated the copying of popular oil paintings on to porcelain. The exceptionally fine fusion of enamel to the soft glaze is a characteristic of Vincennes Sèvres. Fine tableware was modelled by Duplessis, in forms which were influenced by his work on precious metals. Elaborate vases and pots pourris were made with coloured grounds overlaced with gold and decorations after Boucher in the reserves. Forms were pierced and latticed and encrusted with flowers.

Vincennes teapot, c. 1754.

## Sèvres soft-paste (1756–69)

Helped by the interest of Madame de Pompadour, the factory was transferred from Vincennes to a building erected for it at Sèvres. Fine work was done but the factory, forever in financial straits, had to be taken over by the king in 1759. An edict was issued forbidding the making, painting, gilding or even selling of porcelain by any other persons whatsoever. The few factories already working under privilege were permitted to colour in blue only. Pieces from Chantilly and Mennecy of this period are painted *en camaïeu* (in different tones of blue). The severity of this law had to be amended in 1766 and wares in blue and white or *en camaïeu* were allowed to all factories, but not gilding. Figures were forbidden. At Sèvres forms and colour became increasingly rich. In 1757 the *rose Pompadour* ground was introduced and the *bleu de roi* grounds were laced over with such decorations as the *oeil de perdrix* (partridge eye) and the *caillouté* (pebble pattern). In the reserves, military scenes and battles were popular subjects. Tableware, decorative pieces and trinkets were made of such splendour that the king used them as royal gifts in place of the more usual gold and silver. Figures were made in bisque after models by the sculptor, Falconet.

Soft-paste Sèvres,
*trembleuse* cup and
saucer.

## Sèvres hard-paste (1769–74)

Although the secrets of the hard-paste porcelain had been known for some time by the French factories, the apparent absence of a suitable clay in the country made its manufacture unfeasable. The beauty of the soft-paste porcelain and its readiness to take decoration did not make the change to hard-paste urgent but reasons of economy weighed in its favour. Easier to handle in the kiln, there was less wastage and breakage. A search inaugurated in 1769 discovered deposits of kaolin at St Yrieix. From this a hard-paste was produced which was extremely white and opaque, but overglaze colours needed modification to take on the harder surface. Soft-paste continued to be used and vases as much as 30 inches high were made, although much larger pieces were possible in hard-paste. Decoration increasingly covered and obscured the ground but the colours were not so well sunk into the glaze. Ornamental clockcases were made, set in ormolu, and plaques to let into furniture, perhaps more characteristic of the Louis XVI period, were painted. Sculptors of the period were Duplessis, Falconet, Bachelier, La Rue, Bolory and Le Riche and among the many painters were Le Quay, Dodin, Aubert and Asselin. Madame Dubarry was also a patron of the factory.

Hard-paste Sèvres, tureen and cover.

## Sèvres (1774–89)

On the death of Boileau, in the reign of Louis XVI, the factory lost the coordinating hand of its director; however, Queen Marie-Antoinette patronised the factory, and many fine pieces were made at her instigation. She delighted in elegant pieces of inlaid furniture inset with decorated porcelain plaques. Her preference was for small vases to hold a single flower, which were more suitable to her furnishings than the large ornate wares of Sèvres, and many were made for her. The factory was entrusted to the Comte d'Angivillers, and Hettlinger was the chemist. Competition from other factories caused the edicts forbidding the manufacture of porcelain except by Sèvres to be revived but they were hardly heeded and in the Revolution of 1789 these measures were abolished. Earlier styles were still used in the reign of Louis XVI but the essential mood of the period was increasingly classical, inspired by the archaeological discoveries at Pompeii. Detailed copies of well known pictures were painted on plaques and large vases were made part-glazed and part-bisque, mounted in ormolu. Copies of Wedgwood were produced and in 1781 a 'jewel' decoration made of droplets of thick enamel was introduced.

Hard-paste Sèvres, detail of a vase, c. 1781.

Strasbourg group of cherubs, c. 1775.

## Strasbourg (1752–81)

The first factory at Strasbourg was founded by Charles-François Hannong early in the eighteenth century and subsequently run by Paul-Antoine Hannong. This factory, however, was forced to move in 1775, because of the jealously guarded monopoly of the Sèvres factory, and was transferred to Frankenthal. Early Strasbourg and Frankenthal closely resemble each other. In 1766 Joseph-Adam Hannong, son of Paul-Antoine, tried once more to establish a factory for hard-paste porcelain at Strasbourg but difficulty in obtaining a suitable clay and the opposition of the French authorities caused the closure of the factory in 1781, when Hannong left the country heavily in debt. The style of the later factory was Louis Seize. Shapes of tableware show the classical influence of the period and the decoration is finely painted. Apart from figures after models from Vincennes, original work was done both glazed and in bisque but in the former the overglaze is poor both in texture and in colour.

CD

Niderviller tureen and cover.

## Niderviller (from 1765)

At a faience factory he had already established, Baron Jean-Louis de Beyerle, Director of the Strasbourg Mint, first produced porcelain in 1765. Meeting the usual opposition from Sèvres he sold out about 1770 to Adam-Philibert, Comte de Custine, who had the advantage of influence at court. Under Claude François Lanfrey the factory continued until, at his death in 1827, it was taken over by M. L. G. Dryander. Table-wares were largely in the style of the period but much work was also done in the Rococo manner. Landscape decorations were painted in colour and monochrome; ground colours were used with birds and flowers painted in the reserves and scattered flowers were applied to plain grounds. A set of designs illustrating the fables of La Fontaine are of particular interest. Niderviller already had a tradition of figure modelling in the original faience factory where an extra fine body of pipeclay and chalk was used and groups had the delicacy in modelling of porcelain figures. Work done in porcelain was mainly in bisque and the quality rivalled that of Sèvres. Chief modellers were Charles-Gabriel Sauvage and Cofflé who had been at Ottweiller and had owned his own factory at Lunéville.

## Limoges (from 1771)

The kaolin deposits at St Yrieix led to the foundation at Limoges of a porcelain factory by the brothers Grellet and a chemist named Fournier. In 1777 the factory came under the protection of the Compte d'Artois. However the business got into financial difficulties, and in 1784 Gabriel Grellet and his partner Massié succeeded in prevailing upon the king to buy it for the production of hard-paste to be decorated at Sèvres. This factory came to an end in 1796 and the following year another was started which continued until 1854. By this time there were many factories in the area producing good standard commercial tableware. The porcelain had a yellowish tinge and was generally decorated with sprigs of single flowers including the widely used cornflower motif.

Limoges teapot, c. 1870.

Lunéville, two male figures, c. 1770.

## Lunéville (1766–77)

Founded by Paul-Louis Cyfflé, a master modeller, the factory produced hard-paste porcelain of a warm tone, using the clay of St Yrieix. In 1769 an order was made by Sèvres that the wares of the factory should be sold as *terre cuite*; this, after Cyfflé's protest, was modified to *pâte de marbre*. In 1777, after the inevitable financial straits which dogged most porcelain factories of the eighteenth century, Cyfflé left, and in 1780 sold his factory. Most of the moulds went to Niderviller where he was to work as one of their chief modellers. The mark T.D.L., used on work done after 1769, stands for *Terre de Lorraine*. Cyfflé designed bisque groups with subjects appealing to popular sentiment, like Children with a Dead Bird, The Little Sweep, The Stocking Mender, and a group of young lovers, as well as busts of Henry IV and Voltaire. Some of Cyfflé's figures, including The Little Sweep, were copied in porcelain at the factory at Vinovo (Italy) and also in earthenware by some of the Staffordshire potters, who no doubt regarded it as a fair exchange for the large quantities of English-style creamware pottery made at Lunéville.

# Paris

At the end of the eighteenth century innumerable small factories producing hard-paste sprang up in and around Paris under the patronage of various distinguished amateurs of porcelain. Mostly they did no more than ape the wares of Sèvres and, when unmarked, pieces are difficult to ascribe. The more important of these factories were –

## Faubourg St Denis (1777–93)

Started by Pierre-Antoine Hannong, taken over by the Marquis d'Usson in 1776 and under the protection of Charles-Philippe, Comte d'Artois from 1779. The paste is white and translucent and flower bouquets and sprigs are a typical decoration.

## La Courtille: Rue Fontaine-au-Roi (1771–1841)

A factory was founded by Locre and remained in his hands until 1795. It was managed by Laurentius Russinger, who had been *Modellmeister* at Höchst, and was therefore much under the influence of German porcelain. The factory was very productive and figures in bisque were made in quantity.

Faubourg St Denis plate, c. 1785.

### Clignancourt (1771–98)

Founded by Pierre Deruelle, the factory came under the patronage of Louis-Stanislas-Xavier, Comte de Provence, in 1775. Fine porcelain was made under Sèvres influence, and domestic pieces, decorative ware and a few figures were also produced.

### Rue Popincourt (1782–1835)

The factory was started by Johann Nast and was commercially very successful. Tableware and decorative pieces such as clockcases were made, the latter sometimes encrusted with flowers. Figures were also made. Influence came from Sèvres but Wedgwood's jasperware was also copied.

### Fontainebleau (1795)

The factory produced hard-paste porcelain in the manner of the period. Much porcelain, more of commercial than aesthetic value, was produced in the form of decorative pieces and figures.

Clignancourt gilt painted kettle, c. 1760.

NAST
à
PARIS

Tournai bowl, c. 1760.

# BELGIUM

## Tournai (1751 onwards)

With the financial backing of the municipal council and a thirty year monopoly granted by the Empress Marie Thérèse, the manufacture of porcelain was undertaken by François-Joseph Peterinck at a former faience factory at Tournai. There were close associations between Tournai and English factories; English craftsmen worked in the Belgian factory and Nicholas Sprimont of Chelsea came from Liège. Duesbury of Derby copied many bisque figures made at Tournai and in turn that factory, in the nineteenth century, produced many copies of Chelsea.

Tournai ware was at first greyish in tone but as the factory developed and its skill increased, the porcelain was soon fine and of a warm yellow hue. Original in form, it derived its decoration from Meissen and Sèvres, the colours being somewhat paler than the prototypes. A characteristic motif was the 'Cinque bouquets', a large posy of flowers in the middle of a plate with four smaller sprigs on the border. Much blue and white ware was made, including the Meissen onion pattern, and typical of Tournai is a spiral ribbing in the paste. Figures were made resembling those of both Mennecy and the English factories as were groups, designed to be seen in the round with figures arranged round a central tree. Many white pieces made at Tournai were later decorated at The Hague.

Chelsea triangle period,
chinoiserie tea caddy.

# ENGLAND

## Chelsea (from 1745)

Around the year 1745, a porcelain factory was established at
Chelsea, then a riverside village on the outskirts of London.

### Triangle period (1745–49)

Much essential data concerning the factory are missing from
the records but it is known that it was under the direction of a
silversmith, originally from Liège, named Nicholas Sprimont
and a jeweller from France called Charles Gouyn. A good and
translucent soft paste was produced, the colour of which
varied according to the amount of tin oxide which was added
to give it whiteness. The earliest wares contained less and were
inclined to be yellow: their designs were based on the forms of
silverware. Tableware was made and also some figures, mostly
in useful forms such as chinoiseries in the shape of teapots and
incense burners, or models of fish, shells and fruit applied to
salts and jugs. Most pieces were left uncoloured.

Chelsea Raised Anchor fable plate.

## Raised anchor period (1749–52)

In 1749 the Raised Anchor mark was adopted. This did not indicate an immediate departure from the use of the old paste and forms but during the period a change was made in the constitution of the paste by adding bone ash to it, which gave greater stability to the body. Held to the light, circles of extra transparency can be seen which are known as 'Chelsea moons' though they are in fact not peculiar to this factory. Tin oxide was added to the glaze in greater quantities, which can be seen where the glaze pools. A wide variety of new wares was introduced including tablewares and decorative pieces. Some attractive plates painted with subjects from Aesop's fables are attributed to O'Neale. Under the chief modeller, Joseph Willems of Brussels, subjects were adopted from a wide variety of sources including Chinese *Blanc de Chine*, bronzes, Italian pottery groups, paintings and engravings. Figures, which were painted by William Duesbury between 1751 and 1752, were decorated with simplicity, with a wash of colour on a stomacher and sprigging on the folds of the gown.

## Girl-in-the-swing period (1749–54)

This porcelain presents a problem. A number of pieces, of which a model of a girl in a swing is one, have many of the attributes of the Chelsea factory but are thought possibly to have been made by a small break-away factory started by workmen from Chelsea. Charles Gouyn may have had something to do with it as by this time he had severed his connection with that factory. About eighty examples of some twenty-nine models have been identified which appear to have a family resemblance. The paste when analysed shows an unusually high percentage of lead, probably due to powdered glass added to the body. The porcelain is white, sometimes greenish or grey in hue and covered by a shiny glaze. The figures are anatomically simplified but attractively composed. A number of scent bottles are included in the list of pieces attributed to the same factory, which is also credited with being the originator of the fashion for making toys in English factories. The scent bottles and toys were coloured but the figures were left white.

The girl in the swing, c. 1750.

## ed anchor period (1752–58)

y 1752 the Red Anchor mark had come into use. The paste at rst was similar to that of the late Raised Anchor period but a ess translucent body was developed which showed fewer noons'. Less tin oxide was used and the glaze became more ransparent, less white and more liable to crazing. O'Neale ontinued to paint designs from the engravings illustrating esop's fables by Francis Barlow. Designs from the Kakiemon nd from Meissen persisted but a typical Chelsea style evolved 1 the plates decorated with flowers, vegetables, butterflies nd insects. Candelabra, condiment stands, tureens etc. were nade, still using silverware forms with Rococo scrolls and laborations, and a great deal was copied from Vincennes. haracteristic of Chelsea are the tureens, large and small, nodelled in the form of fish, birds, animals, vegetables, lowers and fruit, which are attributed to Joseph Willems. ome scent bottles and toys were made and figures based on Meissen models were translated into more gentle mood, their olours soft and sparingly applied with yellows, pinks, nauves and turquoise predominating. Sets were made of the Arts and Sciences, the Seasons, the Continents and the Senses. ubjects were taken from mythology, and topical figures were nade of sportsmen and women, dancers, street criers, music-ans, monks and nuns and subjects from the Italian Comedy.

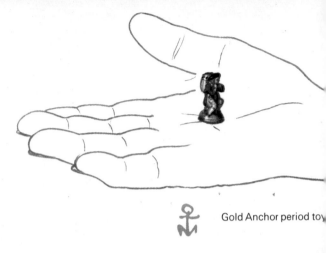

⚓ Gold Anchor period toy

### Gold anchor period (1758–69)

The Gold Anchor mark came into general use in 1758 although a brown anchor was also used as late as the 1760s. The paste of the period, which contained bone ash to render it stronger and less liable to distortion in the firing, was thickly potted and covered by a clear shining glaze which often crazed. The 'mazarine' blue ground which was the equivalent of the *'gros bleu'* of Sèvres, had been experimented with during the Red Anchor period and was now developed. Vases were decorated in the Sèvres manner, with reserves left in the ground colour in which paintings after Boucher were done. Enamellers thought to be working for the factory at this time were John Donaldson of Edinburgh, who was a figure painter, Jeffrey O'Neale who painted subjects from fables and landscapes, and James Giles who painted exotic birds, flowers, and figures in landscape. The figures of the period were extremely ornate and colourful with a lot of gold. Typically English was the development of *bocage*, the leafy background to figures, encrusted with flowers. These groups were to be viewed from the front only, unlike the free-standing figures used for table decoration. Most of the scent bottles in the form of people, birds, animals, baskets of fruit and flowers, boxes in the form of heads, toys, seals and needle cases were made now.

## Chelsea-Derby (1770–84)

Sprimont, for some time in bad health, sold the lease of the Chelsea factory to a James Cox in 1769. Cox sold it to William Duesbury, proprietor of the Derby factory, in the following year and work continued at Chelsea until 1784 when it was transferred to Derby. Early pieces of the period are very similar to Gold Anchor wares in form but two new grounds were introduced in 1771 corresponding to the *'bleu de roi'* and *'bleu céleste'* of Sèvres. Just what was produced at Chelsea and what at Derby is not made clear by the records, as both clay and moulds were sent from one factory to the other and the Gold Anchor mark was still used. A thinner, less lustrous glaze covered the paste at Derby at this time while colours were pale except for an iron-red, and decoration was restrained. Chief modeller was Pierre Stephan; François Gauron, formerly at Tournai, also worked for Chelsea-Derby, as did Jean-Jacques Spengler of Zurich and William Coffee. Figures were copied from French models, some in the style of the bisque figures of Falconet, which had bases of rock formation. Portrait figures were made of eminent persons, after paintings by Neo-classical artists. Around 1770 figures in bisque were exported to France, imperfect specimens being glazed and coloured.

Gold Anchor period vase and cover, c. 1765.

87

## Bow (1746–66)

Near the town of Bow, now part of East London, a porcelain factory was founded in 1746. Patents were granted in 1744 to Edward Heylyn, an Irish painter and portrait artist, and Thomas Frye also a painter, but the earliest date they appear to have marketed their wares is 1746, a year later then Chelsea. They received financial aid from Alderman George Arnold and a suitable china-clay was imported very cheaply from Carolina, America, by Andrew Duché. From the beginning the factory added bone ash to its paste, which gave it the advantage of greater strength and durability than that of its rivals though the glaze was soft and liable to scratches and discoloration. A great deal of experiment with the body seems to have taken place, for early pieces vary from a warm grey hue to a deep cream; later wares are an even creamy-white. Unlike Chelsea wares, which were slip moulded, Bow used the press moulding method which made their figures much heavier. The factory produced quantities of useful wares at reasonable prices. During the illness of Sprimont of Chelsea in 1757, many of the workers of that factory transferred to Bow bringing with them

Bow figure of a gardener, c. 1770.

Bow, blue ground dish, c. 1765.

styles in both painting and modelling which included the use of *bocage*. The factory flourished, at one time employing about 300 workmen of whom 90 were painters.

Early Bow was based on Chinese and Japanese originals but at an early stage developed its own character. Many pieces were made in white, and a pattern commonly used was the raised prunus blossom after the Chinese *Blanc de Chine*. A typical feature of the blue and white ware was the running of the cobalt into the glaze, thus blurring the pattern. Early polychrome pieces were stronger in colour than the later ones. Octagonal wares were made in the Kakiemon style, decorated with the quail pattern, the 'Hedge and Rat', and 'Hob in the Well'. Exotic birds and flowers were used as motifs and naturalistic paintings of botanical specimens were done. Two enamellers working for Bow were James Giles, an outside decorator, and Thomas Craft. Transfer printing, for which Robert Hancock did engravings in the mid 1750s, was used on porcelain, and early figures were mostly adapted from engravings and paintings. Popular actors and actresses, such as Kitty Clive and Henry Woodward, were portrayed in favourite roles, usually in white with square bases. Work done at Bow tended to be more original than at Chelsea and figure subjects were taken from the popular London scene.

Pair of Planché Derby charging bulls.

## Derby (1750–1848)
### Planché (1750–56)

It is thought that porcelain was first made at Derby about the
year 1750, probably by a Frenchman named André Planché.
Evidence is provided by some small uncoloured jugs with the
date 1750 incised upon them and the word Derby or the letter
D. The paste is vitreous and heavy; the glaze, which is a
creamy-white, is inclined to be patchy in parts where it has
missed the body. These early pieces are recognisable by the
'dry edge' where the glaze stops short of the base. The glaze
used was, no doubt, one which ran easily in the firing and was
therefore wiped clear of the bottom to avoid the piece sticking.
Another characteristic is the funnel-shaped hole in the base
left by the slip moulding process. Among pieces made were
well modelled figures of animals, chinoiseries, sets of the
Senses, the Seasons, the Muses, etc. A figure of the actress
Kitty Clive was adapted from the Bow model, and the Meissen
factory was also a source of inspiration. The modelling is
usually rather primitive and the composition of the body is
similar in most respects to the Chelsea body introduced in
1750. Some pieces were coloured, though the majority was
left in white; early figures have heavy pad bases but Rococo
scrolls were added towards the end of the period. At this time
changes in the formula of the porcelain are suggested by the
paste being frequently marred by black speckling.

## Duesbury (1756–70)

In 1756 William Duesbury became a partner in the Derby porcelain factory with André Planché and the financer of the business, John Heath. Planché very shortly left and Duesbury became entirely responsible for the factory. He proved to be a shrewd man of business and organised yearly sales of porcelain. Changes were made in the paste; it became lighter, though it remained vitreous, and the glaze was colder in colour. A method of stacking pieces in the kiln on pads of clay helps to identify the factory, as it left three or four round marks on the bases known as Derby 'patch marks'. Up to 1760 the wares were modelled generally on those of Meissen; after this date the style was based on Chelsea and as wares from that factory sold well a gold anchor was unscrupulously added to some pieces. The Derby factory did not use a mark of its own until the Chelsea-Derby period. In 1770 Duesbury bought up the Chelsea factory and ran the two in conjunction until 1784. (See 'Chelsea-Derby', p. 87.)

Derby, Duesbury figures.

During this period tableware and decorative pieces were made and a distinctive style in flower painting was developed. Sprays of loosely held blossoms were painted in soft colours in which mauve and iron-red were used a great deal; leaves and insects were frequently painted over blemishes in the paste which accounts for their appearance in surprising places. This practice was by no means restricted to the Derby factory. Many figures were made in the Chelsea manner, including a clumsier version of the *bocage* than at Chelsea, and some delightful small animal models were made including some characterful cats on scrolled bases. A variety of birds were produced, perched on white tree trunks with a few applied enamelled flowers and leaves, and mounted on pad bases. A characteristic feature of the Derby base is that the back is solid and does not clear the ground although, from the front, it appears to be mounted on pedestal feet.

Two Duesbury birds.

Duesbury II plate, c. 1780.

## Duesbury II (1786–97)

The Chelsea-Derby factory closed in 1784 and many of the Chelsea workers transferred to Derby. In 1786 Duesbury died and the business was taken over by his son William, known as Duesbury II, in whose hands Derby flourished. Figures continued to be made, more especially the fine biscuit figures for which the factory was renowned, but it is for its painting that Derby of this period is noted. Ground colours were greatly improved, the finest being a canary-yellow, and reserves were left for decoration. The most famous of the enamellers was William Billingsley, who specialised in flowers; in particular he painted pink roses and characteristic of his work is his method of washing in the mass of the flower in colour and removing the highlights with a dampened brush. Zachariah Boreham, formerly of Chelsea, and Thomas (Jockey) Hill painted landscapes, while another painter from Chelsea, who specialised in cupids, was Richard Askew. Birds and fruit were painted by George Complin, and in such men as these Duesbury was fortunate in having some of the finest craftsmen in England working for him.

Quaker Pegg plate, c. 1813.

## Michael Kean (1797–1814)

In 1797 Duesbury II died and the factory continued under the directorship of a painter named Michael Kean who had been taken into partnership two years earlier. He was fortunate in replacing his decorator by William 'Quaker' Pegg, whose flower painting was distinctive. Life-sized blooms in a spray sometimes trail across the plate to the rim, and the name of the flower was written on the reverse side of the piece. He gave up working for the factory in 1800 when he became convinced that his occupation was sinful but returned in 1813, only to leave again in 1820. Painting continued to be done in the Billingsley manner by Moses Webster; other painters were Thomas Steele, who specialised in fruit and flowers; Leonard Lead who painted tulips; Richard Dodson, the bird painter; George Robertson who did land- and seascapes; Robert Brewer, another landscape painter, and a specialist in hunting scenes, Cuthbert Lawton.

# Bloor (1814-48)

Robert Bloor leased the factory from Kean in 1814 and bought the remainder of his stock for £5,000. To pay off this sum, which he had borrowed, he decorated quantities of porcelain which had been set aside as 'seconds' because of flaws. The well known Derby Japan pattern was first used at this period, which covered the ground with rich blues, Indian reds and gilt. The 'Chantilly Sprig' was adapted and, the mood of the day favouring opulent decoration, pieces were made encrusted with flowers. Portrait models were made of eminent persons, and popular figures and characters from fiction, such as Dr Syntax, were also represented by the modellers Samuel and Edward Keys. Porcelain of this period was covered by a poor glaze which had crazed badly and is frequently discolored a yellowish brown.

The original Derby factory closed in 1848; another was started by workmen from the old factory who copied the Derby wares, using some of the original moulds, and in 1935 it was bought up by the present company which had been trading since 1889 under the name of the Royal Crown Derby Porcelain Company Ltd.

Two Bloor figures, c. 1820.

Worcester, Lund gravy boat, c. 1750.

## Worcester (from 1748)

Benjamin Lund (1748–52)

The source of the Worcester factory can be traced to Bristol, where about 1748, at a site now occupied by part of the docks, a factory was established by Benjamin Lund. Lund's formula included a large proportion of soapstone, a substance with a high vitreous content which was an English innovation first used in Bristol. In the letters of a Dr Richard Pococke written in 1750, mention is made of his visit to the Lizard in Cornwall, where he saw 'soapy rock . . . which is mostly valued for making porcelain'. Lund himself had obtained the first licence recorded for quarrying the substance.

Few of the wares of this shortlived factory appear to have survived and only some thirteen are known to have the name 'Bristoll' embossed on the base. The porcelain was a soft-paste of fine quality, well potted, with Rococo mouldings and flutings; the glaze was greyish and decoration was done in blue and white and polychrome. Mauve, blue, green, yellow and iron-red were used for designs derived from the Chinese *famille verte* and *famille rose* etc. and the Japanese Kakiemon. A Chinese figure after a *Blanc de Chine* model has the date 1750 on the base. Later designs were European in style.

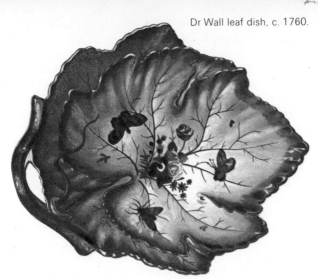

## Dr Wall (1751–83)

On 4th June 1751, a deed of partnership was drawn up between fifteen people who founded the Worcester Porcelain Company. Of these partners the most important was Dr John Wall and it is his name which has been given to the wares produced up to the year 1783, although the Doctor died in 1776. Other signatories of note were Richard Holdship, who secured the future supplies of soap rock, his brother Josiah, William Davis, William Bayliss, and Edward Cave, the editor of the 'Gentleman's Magazine', through which the company was able to advertise its goods. The formula for the porcelain was bought from the Bristol factory and its secrets appear to have been in the hands of two workmen, Robert Podmore and John Lyes, both of Bristol. Finely made wares were produced which included fluted dishes and plates with scalloped edges, Rococo moulded jugs with raised patterns, pickle dishes in the form of leaves, baskets, teapots, hexagonal vases, cauliflower and partridge tureens on leaf stands and so on. Many pieces were based on silver forms. The body and glaze united perfectly and never crazed, though a pitting and speckling sometimes occurred. The glaze on the base of the later wares of the period has often shrunk away a little from the footrim.

Many pieces were decorated in blue and white using a dark cobalt underglaze which sometimes drifted a little into the glaze. Flowers were painted first in the Chinese manner and later in a European style and on moulded wares the pattern wanders across without making much attempt to accommodate the raised pattern. The blue and white wares of Caughley are commonly mistaken for Worcester, especially as they both used the C mark. Worcester porcelain, however, usually transmits a green colour when held to the light, and Caughley a brown one. In polychrome pieces the colours are fresh and bright and a soft gold was sparingly used. Early painters are mostly unknown by name but a plate with a painting of a bird is dated 1757 and signed by James Rogers. In the same year Worcester adopted the use of transfer prints for some of their wares; their originator, Robert Hancock, had worked at the Battersea enamel factory and later at Bow. It was, however, at Worcester that the method of printing in black was developed. Best known examples are the mugs featuring a portrait of Frederick the Great; others were done of George II, George III, Queen Charlotte, William Pitt and the Marquess of Granby. Subjects included children's games, chinoiseries, birds, ruins in landscapes, The Tea Party and scenes of gallantry.

Transfer printed mug, 1757.

Worcester jug with
scale-blue ground, c. 1770.

In 1764, owing to the ill-health of Sprimont, work at the
Chelsea factory was disrupted and many of its workers came
to Worcester. Typical decoration of the period was the scale-
blue ground in which reserves were left for decoration with
flowers, fruit, birds, landscapes and scenes with figures.
Overglaze grounds were also used, one of the finest and rarest
being yellow. Worcester developed its own interpretation of
Japanese designs which became known as 'Worcester Japan
Patterns' in which iron-reds, greens and dark blues predominated, and formalised garlands and diaper patterns were used.
O'Neale, the independent decorator, painted scenes from
Aesop's fables, panels of hunting scenes and figure subjects
from the Italian Comedy on hexagonal vases etc., while other
decorators were Giles, John Donaldson and Pillement. Tablewares were enamelled with elaborate coats of arms. Worcester
figures are rare and the few that were made were stiff and
doll-like and rather naively modelled, sometimes on pad bases
with applied flowers, or a scroll and shell motif, sometimes on
Rococo pedestal feet. One modeller thought to have been
responsible for figure modelling was Tebo.

*Chamberlains Worcester*

Chamberlain cachepot.

## Flight factories (1783–1840)

In 1776 Dr Wall died and the factory carried on under the direction of William Davis. For identification purposes the period referred to as 'Dr Wall' by collectors is extended to 1783, when Davis died and the factory was bought by Thomas Flight. A change made in the paste produced a whiter porcelain and the old honey gold was replaced by the brassier mercury gilding. Detailed topographical scenes were painted, sometimes on plaques cast with a surrounding frame, and the shell and feather motif was exquisitely painted on pieces such as coffee cans intended more for cabinet display than for use. Usually well marked, the porcelain was of a greyer hue at this time; spill vases with ring handles were among typical pieces made. During the years 1783–1840, the factory changed its name with the changing partnerships, becoming Flight & Barr in 1792, Barr Flight & Barr in 1807 and Flight Barr & Barr from 1813 to 1840.

## Chamberlain (1800–40)

A second Worcester factory had been set up in 1786 by Robert Chamberlain. At first it only decorated porcelain for Caughley but soon produced much the same wares as the Flight factory, except that they lacked a lightness in form and decoration. The factory prospered and in 1840 took over the original company, Flight Barr & Barr.

## Longton Hall (1749–60)

This factory is one of those whose history is still being pieced together and the identification of its products are sometimes a matter of dispute. Founded in the potteries by 'William Jenkinson, gentleman' and two partners, the factory used a paste, the secret of which was probably brought from London. The influence of salt glaze pottery can also be seen, especially in the surprisingly bright blue often used very broadly, known as Littler's blue. Both pottery and porcelain share a characteristic addition of gilding. Though prolific the factory was never a financial success. Earliest experimental wares are thought to have been figures in the style of existing pottery and salt glaze pieces. A thick vitreous glaze, blurring the form, has earned them the name of 'Snowmen'. Moulded tablewares were made in blue and in polychrome, and typical products were plates in strawberry leaf form, Rococo vases with raised scrollwork and twisted rope handles, sauceboats in silverware forms and boxes in the shape of fruits. All the sophisticated forms of continental porcelain were used, but though fine work was done the influence of pottery persisted and there is often a certain naivety in interpretation.

Longton Hall figure of a cabbage seller.

## Lowestoft (c. 1757–c. 1802)

The Lowestoft factory was founded in 1757 by three men, Walker, Aldred and Richman, whose interests had hitherto been mainly in the fishing industry. Wares owed little to contemporary English porcelain, being based rather on salt glaze and other pottery and the simpler forms of Chinese pieces. The body was of a creamy colour, the glaze greenish or tinged with blue, according to the presence of copper or cobalt in the underglaze decoration which had a tendency to spread into the glaze. There is an endearing homeliness to the wares, which include pieces inscribed 'A trifle from Lowestoft' with the initials or name of the receiver, or the name of the inn for which it was ordered. They were intended to grace the tavern and the tradesman's table and were offered at '20 per cent allowance for ready money'. Wares included birth commemoration tablets, ink-wells, mugs, pap warmers and tea and coffee pots. Early pieces are in blue and white but after 1770 polychrome wares were made in which a mauvy pink predominated. Lowestoft was not responsible for the so-called Chinese Lowestoft porcelain, armorial pieces exported from China but still known by that name, especially in America.

Lowestoft, Milk jug, and Inkpot.

# Liverpool (c. 1754–99)

At Shaw's Brow, on the hills rising from Merseyside, a colony of potters grew up in the mid eighteenth century. There had been no tradition of pottery at Liverpool but, until excavation proved otherwise, the wares of several of these factories were mistaken at times for those of Longton Hall and Worcester. Benefiting by the experience of the already established English factories, those of Liverpool used a vitreous paste and also pastes containing bone ash and soapstone. Wares were made for utility rather than ornament, chiefly in blue and white. Little is known of most of the factories but something is recorded of Richard Chaffers and his partners. Early porcelain was greyish, well potted with neat rims to the base, decorated in an underglaze blue which blurred into the glaze, and in polychrome. Podmore introduced soapstone into the paste, producing a chalk-white colour, and used a wet-looking glaze. Cups and mugs with flat bases have characteristically bevelled edges. Decoration and colour improved and some printed wares were made as well as mask-lipped jugs and punch bowls. Transfer printing was used, a ship motif being popular, and tablewares were decorated with raised scrollwork.

Liverpool sauceboat.

2

Plymouth figure of a goat, c. 1768.

## Plymouth (1768–1773)

The factory at Plymouth was shortlived, but had the distinction of being the first English factory to use hard-paste. The secrets of its manufacture were not brought from the continent but were the discovery of its founder, an apothecary with an inquiring mind, William Cookworthy. He found a friend and supporter in Lord Camelford on whose grounds the materials for the porcelain were discovered. Difficulty in achieving a consistency in the paste made the venture unprofitable, and in 1773 the project was abandoned in Plymouth. The factory removed to Bristol where it was more possible to recruit knowledgeable technicians and workmen. Difficulties with the Plymouth paste made flatwares impractical and account for distortions in other pieces; upright wares such as mugs proved easier. Typical of the factory are the spiral throwing marks left by the potter's fingers. Numerous sauceboats in silverware forms were made, with Rococo mouldings; cups were frequently decorated in underglaze blue, while M. Soqui, a French enameller, painted exotic birds in polychrome. Large decorative vases were made, as were dishes, ornamented with applied shells and models of animals. The glaze, however, was frequently marred by smokiness.

Bristol figure of a goatherd,
c. 1775.

# Bristol (1774–81)

The patent of the former Plymouth factory was transferred to
Richard Champion in 1774. A younger man than Cookworthy,
he was an established merchant in Bristol who gave his en-
thusiasm and energy to the establishment of the factory and
made great improvements in the porcelain. However in
obtaining an extension of fourteen years to his lease, which was
opposed by Josiah Wedgwood, he was involved in litigation
which led to financial ruin and the closure of the factory.
With a more malleable paste a great range of wares were
produced, mostly for domestic use, and the factory developed
its own distinctive style. Four shapes of cup were made: the
straight-sided coffee can, the tea bowl without handle, the
U-shaped cup and a wider topped cup with curved sides.
Wares were sometimes fluted and teapots were made with
large handles and rather short spouts. Wreaths and festoons,
sometimes enclosing cameo heads or initials, are a typical
decoration. Plaques of flowers were modelled in white biscuit and handsome garnitures of hexagonal vases were
produced. Pieces for general sale were decorated mainly with
natural flowers; more opulent services were Neo-classical with
formalised designs, armorial devices and rich gilding.

## New Hall (1782–c. 1835)

In 1781 the patents of the Bristol factory were sold by Richard Champion to a company which founded a factory at Shelton Hall, later known as New Hall, in 1782, under the management of John Daniel. Early wares closely resembled Bristol as a similar clear milk-white porcelain was made, but the glaze differed somewhat, tending to pool and to leave dry patches on the paste. Mainly domestic pieces such as tea and coffee services were made then, after the first few years, the factory went in for mass production and short cuts led to more arbitrary potting. Earlier wares were decorated with Chinese figures and landscapes, or European pastoral scenes and at least one outside decorator, Fidèle Duvivier, who painted in both monochrome and polychrome, was used. Tablewares were banded with decoration at rim and foot and sprigged with flowers; enamelling was sometimes done over a printed outline. Earlier forms show a diversity but later shapes became standardised, and oval and narrow rectangular teapots were made on stands to match. Later productions of the factory follow the prevailing taste, and decorative motifs were shared with other Staffordshire potteries; however, pieces after about 1812 usually have a factory mark to indicate their origin.

New Hall chinoiserie saucer.

## Caughley or Salopian ware (1772–1814)

In Shropshire, on the banks of the Severn close to Ironbridge, a pottery was established in 1751 by a Mr Gallimore, whose daughter married Thomas Turner who had worked at the Worcester factory. In 1772 Turner took over the Caughley factory for the manufacture of porcelain, and in 1783 established the 'Salopian China warehouse' in London. Caughley decoration was mostly in underglaze blue, usually printed, with a frequent addition of gilding. Worcester patterns were copied, which can make identification difficult, especially as glaze shrinkage on the base is also visible, but the porcelain shows a brownish yellow when held to the light, whereas Worcester transmits a greenish hue; exceptions to this rule are not common. To Caughley is ascribed the origin of the Willow Pattern derived originally from the Chinese; the legend attached to the Willow Pattern is a purely English invention. Typical of the factory were trellis baskets, with rosettes at the interstices, and mask-lipped jugs with round bodies and straight necks. Robert Hancock worked at Caughley for a short time and some polychrome wares were made. In 1799 finding competition from the Stafford potteries too great, Turner sold his lease to Coalport.

C
S<sub>x</sub>

Caughley mug, c. 1785.

*G Dale*

Coalport swan-neck vase.

## Coalport (from 1799)

The Caughley factory was run by John Rose in conjunction with his already established business at Coalport (known also as Coalbrookdale). In 1814 Caughley was closed and its equipment transferred to Coalport. A good business man, Rose established outlets for his wares through London dealers, and by 1820 he had incorporated the factory of Swansea and by 1828 that of Nantgarw. To Rose goes the credit of introducing leadless glaze which eliminated the previous hazard to the health of pottery workers.

Early pieces continued in the established style of Caughley and white wares were made for decoration at the Coalport factory, and also sold to outside decorators such as Thomas Pardoe of Bristol. Imitations were made of Chelsea, Worcester, and more especially of Sèvres, including the *rose Pompadour* ground. A maroon and a deep rich underglaze blue ground are typical of Coalport while many flower-encrusted pieces were made. Ink-wells, vases, comports, clock cases, dishes and candlesticks were lavishly ornamented with painted decoration and applied mouldings.

# Davenport: Longport (1793–1882)

A factory already established at Longport was taken over by a Mr Davenport in 1793 and was run by members of his family until 1882. It produced domestic wares for a mass market but also included such services for official use as the one made for the coronation of William IV, and one commemorating the Union of Great Britain and Ireland. On this the national emblems, joined by the Union Jack, were the central decorative motif which was surrounded by a border of apple-green with flower painting in the reserves, and gilding. Tea services and decorative dessert sets with comports are typical of the factory. Wares of Derby, Swansea and Rockingham, and more particularly of Sèvres, were copied and a *rose Pompadour* ground was used; some rather absurd Rococo vases are also found with the firm's mark. Thomas Steele of Derby worked at Davenport as enameller for a time and probably the painter James Rouse, who worked in the water-colour manner of Birkett Foster. The factory also produced a stoneware for the cheaper market.

Davenport jug, c. 1830.

## Pinxton (1796–1813)

The factory at Pinxton was started by William Billingsley, chief flower painter from Derby, where he had been an apprentice under Duesbury. A John Coke, who had an estate at Pinxton, had found clay there which he had suggested to Duesbury might be used in the manufacture of porcelain, but failed to interest him. Billingsley had been making experiments of his own to produce a finer body and persuaded Coke to build a factory, and allow him to produce porcelain, from the profits of which he would be paid. In 1799 Billingsley left and Pinxton continued under the direction of William Coffee, a modeller from Derby, then in 1806 Coke leased the factory to John Cutts, an enameller. Identification of Pinxton is difficult: three types of paste were used: a copy of the Derby body, Billingsley's fine translucent white paste, thinly potted, and later, under Cutts, a heavier porcelain. Tea and coffee pots were made with square handles, and tableware vases, spill vases and some handsome crocus pots, possibly decorated by Billingsley himself, were produced. Canary-yellow and salmon-pink grounds were used and views of country seats, topographical scenes and churches were painted in medallions. Flower painting was of a high standard.

Pinxton yellow-ground ice pail, c. 1810.

## Minton's (from 1796)

The factory was founded at Stoke-on-Trent in 1796 by Thomas Minton, an engraver who had worked under Turner at Caughley, and also at Spode. In 1836 a John Boyle became a partner whereupon the factory became Minton and Boyle: Boyle left after five years to join Wedgwood's, and Minton's nephews entered the firm. The factory produced a semi-transparent ware until 1821, when a soft white paste was used which compared favourably with that of the other English factories. Pieces were made in contemporary styles and earlier wares were reproduced. At the time of the Great Exhibition of 1851 a fine new white body was introduced and excellent copies of early Sèvres were made. Typical of Minton's was the use of a turquoise ground colour and decorative gilding, though of course a range of other ground colours were used. The most interesting contribution to English ceramics was the work of Marc-Louis Solon who came to Mintons in 1870 from Sèvres. He had developed a new technique of decoration, the *pâte-sur-pâte*, which used a white slip over a coloured ground so that it had a cloudy semi-transparent appearance. Nymphs and classical figures with floating draperies lent themselves particularly as subjects to this type of work.

SPODE
NEW STONE

Spode comport, c. 1820.

## Spode (1800 to the present)

The first Josiah Spode was a potter. Originally apprenticed to Thomas Whieldon, he started on his own at Stoke-on-Trent in 1770. His son Josiah II produced porcelain at the factory in 1800, where he was the first to use a type of bone china which was to be copied by the leading English factories from then on. In 1813 William Copeland became a partner and greatly developed the business to an impressive size. Josiah II died in 1827 and his son Josiah III succeeded him and in 1833 Copeland's son bought the business and Thomas Garrett joined the firm as a partner.

Spode porcelain was soft, white, well potted and very translucent. Copies were made of Nantgarw, Swansea, Chelsea, Meissen, early Sèvres and the Chinese but such pieces were clearly marked. The factory made a great deal of blue and white ware, particularly of the Willow Pattern, the origin of which has been ascribed to Caughley. Domestic pieces were made in quantity, including miniature tea services for children. At Copeland's factory Parian ware, an unglazed body with a translucent quality comparable to Parian marble which lent itself to the reproduction of statuary, was invented and was quickly copied by other factories. A paste known as Feldspar porcelain was also introduced by Spode, the secret of which was kept from competitors. Indeed it was such a well kept secret that it has since been altogether lost.

## Nantgarw and Swansea (1813–22)

The factory of Nantgarw was founded by the restless William Billingsley, who had worked at Derby, Pinxton and Worcester and as an outside decorator. He had always been deeply interested in improving the formula for porcelain and by 1813 had established a small factory in Glamorganshire with his son-in-law Samuel Walker. He had no capital to develop the business and applied for a government grant. A factory at Swansea was put at his disposal and he and Walker moved there. When, however, there came to light the breach of contract of these two potters with their former employers at Worcester, the Swansea factory was closed to them and they returned to Nantgarw in 1817. For three years they managed to carry on and then sold the formula to Coalport. Billingsley's paste was vitreous and brilliantly white; the glaze was excellent and the potting fine; flower painting was of the highest standard, though the most ambitious pieces were sent to London for decoration. Working for the factory were Thomas Pardoe, William Weston Young, John Latham and William Pegg.

(*right*) Nantgarw spill vase, c. 1800.
(*left*) Swansea cup, c. 1780.

SWANSEA

## Rockingham (Swinton) (1826–42)

In 1806 Thomas Brameld and his son William became the proprietors of a pottery already established at Swinton, on the estate of Earl Fitzwilliam, Marquis of Rockingham. From 1820 two younger Bramelds experimented with a formula for porcelain and in 1826 went into production. The griffin mark, derived from the Rockingham coat of arms, was adopted, and the firm became the Royal Rockingham Works after it had made a fine dessert service for William IV in 1830. The porcelain contained bone ash and was white, translucent and substantial, having a tendency to very fine crazing. Typical pieces were vases with wide trumpet-shaped lips, floral baskets with rustic handles, pots pourris, inkstands, and tea and dessert services. The style was an adaption of Rococo, with copious use of scrolls and applied flowers, while ground colours were in a variety of shades of blue, green and red. A curious grey ground was peculiar to the factory and both glazed and biscuit figures were made but are quite rare. Models were made of European peasants in national costume and Meissen monkey musicians were copied. A curiosity is a replica of a pilgrim by Gardner of Moscow which presumably was made after George Frederick Brameld's visit to St Petersburg.

Rockingham plate, c. 1820, and figure, c. 1830 (copy of a Russian model by Gardner).

Mason plate, c. 1830.

## Miles Mason (1800–13)

Miles Mason was a potter and a dealer in porcelain and glass, and owned a shop in Fenchurch Street, London, which he opened in 1780. Duties imposed on the import of porcelain were responsible for the closure of his business and he turned to the production of wares at a factory which he established in Market Street, Fenton, and later removed to the Minerva works in the same town.

He made excellent hard-paste porcelain and bone china, decorated mostly in the Oriental manner with blues and reds predominating; gilt was sometimes applied to the more ambitious pieces. Printing was mainly used, sometimes in pale underglaze blue, sometimes in black stipple, and enamelling was also done. In 1813 Miles Mason retired and his son C. J. Mason, who carried on the business, patented 'Ironstone China' which should not be confused with the earlier porcelain produced by his father.

Wedgwood basalt teapot.

## Wedgwood (1759 to the present)

Since Josiah Wedgwood produced little true porcelain it is debatable whether he should be introduced into a book devoted to that subject; however, his influence on European porcelain was enormous, and his stoneware of such a quality as to vie with the finest porcelain. He was the originator of mass production, developing world-wide markets and becoming a serious threat to rival potteries at home and abroad. His earliest productions were his elegantly formed creamwares, finer than the earthenware used by those who could not afford porcelain, and therefore finding a ready market. Queen Charlotte, presented with a Wedgwood breakfast set and caudle on the birth of a child, was so delighted with it as to allow it henceforth to be called Queen's ware. After making some less interesting pieces in a buff stoneware, Wedgwood produced his black basalt which was a dense, smooth, unglazed body suitable for casting decorative pieces in the classical style. This was sometimes coloured in what Wedgwood called encaustic painting, a fired colour and not a coloured wax. In 1769 Wedgwood took into partnership Thomas Bentley, to whom credit must be given for encouraging his interest in the excavations at Herculaneum.

## Wedgwood and Bentley (1769-80)

A direct result of the classical revival was the naming of the factory Etruria which was founded in Burslem, Staffordshire. The publication in 1766 of a catalogue of Sir William Hamilton's collection of Greek antiquities was a source of inspiration to Wedgwood, who made copies of some of the black and red vases. He became extremely interested in the work of Robert Adam and his delicate adaptations of classical motifs, for he saw that friezes and decorations in plaster relief could equally well be interpreted in ceramics. In 1774 experiments produced a new body, a porcellaneous stoneware named jasperware. In this the white frieze was cast separately from the coloured ground on to which it was laid. The relief work was then sharpened by skilful tooling, although later wares lack this refinement. In the early wares the ground is coloured throughout; later a coating of colour was applied. Blue was the most common colour, but sage-green, yellow and lavender were used. A wide variety of wares were made, from fonts to inlaid fireplaces, tablewares, vases, and plaques for insetting into pianos, clocks, mirrors, torchères and furniture.

Decorative urns, statuettes and busts were manufactured, and sometimes sets for decorating chimneypieces, which included all these, were produced. Figures from classical

Three-colour plaque.

A scent bottle.

A chess piece.

mythology, sphinxes and griffins were made, sometimes free-standing, sometimes supporting such objects as candlesticks and candelabra. The nature of the material lent itself to use with other materials such as marble, crystal, ormolu and wood. Innumerable small pieces were made such as pulls for window blinds and bells, door furniture, jewellery and buttons. Flaxman designed a chess set, of which the king and queen are said to resemble Kemble and Mrs Siddons. Another modeller of importance was William Hackwood. Pieces were made in biscuitware for ladies to decorate for amusement in their own homes, and elegant colour boxes and palettes were made for them in the same material. Bentley died in 1780; he had been a close friend and collaborator of Wedgwood to whom his death was a great loss. A sale was held in 1781 to realise Mrs Bentley's share in her husband's partnership and the catalogue of this auction has been invaluable in the dating and identification of pieces. Some experiments with true porcelain were done in 1776 with clay from China, but not until 1812 was it made in any quantity. From then till 1822 bone porcelain was made, but the main production was basalt and jasperwares.

Wedgwood copy of the
Portland Vase.

## The Portland Vase

The most ambitious pieces ever made by Josiah Wedgwood
were his copies of the Portland Vase. This was a unique
example of Greek cameo-glass in the possession of the Duke of
Portland, which was later to be shattered into fragments by an
eccentric while it was on public view in the British Museum in
1845. Wedgwood estimated that £5,000 would not cover the
costs of the undertaking, so he decided to make several
qualities of copy, to be ordered by advance subscription. The
material of the original was a dark blue glass overlaid with
white, the top layer being cut in the manner of a cameo into a
classical frieze. Wedgwood proposed to make some pieces cast
simply in one colour, some with the blue ground painted in
and others with the blue part made of jasperware which, in
the more expensive pieces, would be polished. The finest
examples were worked upon by an engraver. Chief modeller
was Henry Webber with William Wood and William Hackwood working on the designs. The Portland Vase was loaned
to Wedgwood for a year but it took three years' work, from
1786 to 1789, before a copy completely satisfied Wedgwood.

Belleek basket, c. 1880.

## IRELAND

### Belleek (from 1863)

The first attempt to produce porcelain at Belleek was made by John Caldwell Bloomfield, owner of the Castle Caldwell estate in Fermanagh. Interest in the brilliance of the white-washed walls of a local cottage led to his discovery that his whole estate lay on a bed of feldspar clay. A small factory was started to produce porcelain but failed and soon closed. Kerr, of the Royal Porcelain factory, went to Ireland, accompanied by the firm's architect, Robert Armstrong, to prospect for suitable materials which might be imported for use at the Worcester factory. Armstrong was extremely impressed with the results of experiments carried out at Worcester with the feldspar from the Belleek district mixed with china clay from Cornwall. In cooperation with David McBirney of Dublin, he built a factory on an island on the river Erne, on the borders of Donegal and Fermanagh, where production started in 1863. Workers were brought from England, with about a dozen from the Goss factory, including its foreman William Bromley, and a fine modeller, William W. Gallimore. A story is told of Gallimore that he lost his right arm in an accident with a gun, but subsequently modelled even better with his left!

The factory at first traded under the name of D. McBirney & Co. It produced a soft-paste porcelain with a thick iridescent glaze which gave the mother-of-pearl lustre peculiar to Belleek. The business prospered and received royal patronage. Queen Victoria commissioned a presentation tea service for the Empress of Austria, the design for which was based on a sea-urchin standing on a branch of coral. The factory continued to seek inspiration for its forms in marine life, shells of all kinds, sea gods and goddesses and all the flora and fauna of the ocean bed figuring widely. An immensely elaborate table service in the Victorian taste was also made for the Prince of Wales. Some pieces were made part in Parian, a white marble-like biscuit, and part in the nacreous lustre glaze. An ice pail was designed with raised figures of tritons blowing on gilded conches as they disport amongst the reeds, and with the rim resembling coral and the base in the form of a shell. The stem, consisting of three entwined mermaids, was made in Parian; the lid was decorated with seahorses rising from a tumultuous sea and surmounted by a triton riding on a dolphin. Cups and saucers were made in paper-thin egg-shell china for display in cabinets and finely potted fragile baskets were produced sometimes encrusted with delicate flowers. As in so much work of the period, aesthetic taste lagged behind fine craftsmanship and later wares became increasingly vulgar.

Belleek shells, c. 1870.

## HOLLAND

### Weesp (1759–71)

The first porcelain factory in Holland was at Weesp, near
Amsterdam, founded by Count van Gronsveldt Diepenbroi
at a former earthenware pottery. The factory came under both
German and French influence, employing workmen from both
countries. For a time Nikolaus Paul, formerly an arcanist a
Wegely's factory in Berlin who had also worked at Fürsten
berg, was at Weesp. There is a saucer in the Victoria and Alber
Museum in London which is decorated with a painted figure o
Pantaloon, a character from the Italian Comedy, which i
recognisable as being derived from a Fürstenberg model b
Feilner. The porcelain was hard-paste, beautifully potted an
of a creamy-white colour tending sometimes to brown. Form
were in the Rococo style with applied scrolls and mouldings
and decorations were done of flowers, exotic birds, landscape
and figure groups. Overglaze was sometimes dark in colour bu
there was some lively flower painting in puce with pal
yellow, green and blue touches, delicately and finely done
diaper and scale patterns were also used. A few figures wer
made, mostly left uncoloured.

Weesp bowl, c. 1767.

M.O.L
✳

ude Loosdrecht plaque, c. 1775.

## Oude Loosdrecht (1771–84)

art of the factory of Weesp was transferred after its closure
o Oude Loosdrecht, where another was started by Johannes
e Mol, a Calvinist minister. In 1774 he took as partner Louis-
ictor Gerverot who had formerly worked at Weesp. The
orcelain was an improvement on that of the earlier factory,
eing whiter with a finer surface. Forms were in the current
ouis Seize manner but also showed some originality, such as
ne elongated thistle-shaped vases on square bases, the top
alf of which was of delicately potted basketwork, decorated
/ith gilt, and the body painted with flowers. As might be
xpected of the Dutch, fine paintings were done of landscapes,
eascapes, still-lifes, waterfowl and genre subjects. These
/ere painted with a rich depth and use of tone which gave the
/ares an exceptional quality. Few figures were produced but
·usts in biscuit on plinths, which were sometimes glazed, were
1ade after the fashion of Sèvres.

## Amstel (1784–1810)

The factory of Oude Loosdrecht was transferred in 1784 to Amstel where it was put under the direction of a German, Friedrich Däuber. The porcelain made was of an excellent quality. The moulds originally made by the factory at Oude Loosdrecht were still used and some of the original workmen were employed by the company. Pieces were made in the fashionable styles of the period and the factory did not produce much that was original. Teapots with rectangular handles might be picked out as most typical of Amstel.

Amstel
M.O.L.

Amstel cup and saucer of about
1800, each decorated with a
design of peasants in a rural scene.

Teapot decorated at The Hague, c. 1775.

## The Hague (c. 1776–90)

The factory at The Hague was founded by a German dealer in porcelain, Anton Lynker of Leichuer, who was also engaged in the enamelling of imported plain wares. The stork mark of The Hague, when it is in overglaze, is often to be found on porcelain of other factories; soft-paste treated in this way is usually Tournai, and sometimes the A of Ansbach is concealed. Lynker had built himself a large home market and even exported to Turkey, becoming a serious rival to the factory of Oude Loosdrecht whose wares his own closely resembled. Though less varied in form than that factory's his wares reached a high standard in both paste and decoration. Among many fine enamellers were Leonardus Temminck, a miniature painter who specialised in subjects from Boucher *en camaieu*, and de Saint-Ligie, a pupil of Greuze. The porcelain was Neo-classical in style and mostly intended for use. Landscapes, figures, birds, flowers and classical heads *en grisaille* were used as decoration, all painted in a highly competent manner.

# RUSSIA

## St Petersburg (Russian Imperial Factory) (from c. 1744)

Early in the century, Peter the Great brought a foreigner named Eggerbank to St Petersburg to experiment with the making of porcelain, but presumably without success. An expedition was later sent to China in the hope that the secrets of its manufacture might be obtained, if necessary by bribery. If the formula was given it was not well enough understood, for it was not until the middle of the century that porcelain is known to have been produced. In 1744 Dmitri Vinogradov was appointed by Elizabeth to supervise the research and by 1750 was producing domestic pieces followed soon by boxes for snuff and some *trompe l'oeil* boxes in the form of addressed envelopes. Figures were also made, among them blackamoors, allegorical subjects and chess pieces, under the influence of Meissen and Berlin. Early porcelain of St Petersburg varied in quality; the more ambitious pieces were of good paste but more general wares were frequently dull and yellowish in glaze.

St Petersburg stippled figure, c. 1780.

Catherine II made it her business to see that the secrets of both paste and enamel were in the possession of Russian workmen so that the work was not disrupted by the departure of foreign craftsmen. Influence was now predominantly from Sèvres and Vienna and the style Neo-classical. Sumptuous prestige services for banquets were made, the famous Arabesque service being of 1,000 pieces, and armorial pieces were popular. A foremost enameller was Dominique Rachette. As time progressed the porcelain took on a more national character mainly through its decoration; topographical views were used and portraits of Catherine were in vogue. During the reign of Paul I figures were made of peasants in regional costume, and experiments were made with biscuit-ware. By the time of Alexander I the porcelain was generally concealed entirely by decoration and tooled gilt. Views of towns and palaces were frequently applied and in the reign of Nicholas I regimental and military scenes, surrounded by wide bands of tooled gilt very typical of Russia, were commonly illustrated. Characteristic grounds were violet and dark blue.

Plate with military scene, c. 1835.

*C*

Moscow figure by Gardner

## Moscow (1765–1891)

The chief porcelain factory to be found at Moscow was established by an Englishman named Francis Jacob Gardner. It is
known that he arrived in Russia in 1746 but nothing is
recorded of his earlier history. He began experiments to find
a satisfactory formula for his paste in the 1750s, and by 1765
he was already in production at Verbilki, near Moscow. Later
he started another factory at Tver, not far away, and some
faience was also produced. Much of the porcelain was in the
style of St Petersburg and followed the current fashion of the
European factories. The influence of Wedgwood was introduced by Lord Cathcart, the British Consul, who took a
selection of Wedgwood ware to Russia to show the Empress
Catherine, and gained an order for an Imperial dinner service
for the English factory in 1773. Among the most interesting of
the earlier Gardner pieces are some fish boxes painted with
great realism. With time the porcelain began to evolve a
character which is recognisably Russian.

Large dinner services were made with great elaboration, some of which were commissioned by the Empress and decorated with insignia of Russian orders of chivalry. Colours were bright to the point of being gaudy and very wide bands of solid gilt, engraved with patterns, decorated the rims and feet of much of the later wares, with landscapes and scenes with figures filling the space between-Characteristic of the 1820s is the elongated shape of cups, jugs, coffee pots etc. with the handle swept high and ending in a flourishing loop. Particularly representative of Gardner's factory are his figures. Many subjects were taken from peasant life, street sellers, such as a Woman with a Basket or a Man Breaking the Ice. They were mostly in biscuit, the colouring matt, very simply painted in strong colours with blue often used in association with black accents on hat and feet. The factory was finally absorbed by the Kuznetsov factories at Dulev in 1891. A charming item of porcelain, produced by most of the Russian factories in the nineteenth century, was in the form of an Easter egg, a traditional Russian present on Easter day.

Figure by Gardner, c. 1815.

Marieberg tea caddy, c. 1773

# SWEDEN

## Marieberg (1758–88)

On an island which has now become part of Stockholm, a factory for the production of both pottery and porcelain was started in 1758 by the royal dentist, J. E. L. Ehrenreich, who was under the patronage of King Adolphe Frederick of Sweden, with Johann Buchwald from Rörstrand as manager.

Fire destroyed the original factory and in 1766 Pierre Berthevin, who had worked at Mennecy and Copenhagen, succeeded Ehrenreich. The factory at this time was producing soft-paste porcelain very much in the manner of Mennecy. During Berthevin's time work was done on transfer printing. In 1769 he left for Frankenthal and his place was taken by Henrik Sten who introduced hard-paste. His porcelain, however, had the appearance of a creamy coloured earthenware although in form and decoration it kept to the original character of the factory. The Marieberg colours were clear and brilliant.

Custard cup with lid, c. 1765.

Between 1777 and 1778 a French arcanist, Jacob Dorter, introduced a hard-paste more akin to the European type. When he left the factory it seems that he took his secrets with him and the old paste was once more produced. Marieberg forms and decorations are narrow in range; early pieces were Rococo in style and later became Neo-classical. Neat little custard cups with lids, decorated with spiral reeding, and painted with sprays of flowers and predominantly pink in colour, must have been made in surprisingly large quantities. Figures were also made and, as might be expected, they followed the Mennecy style and choice of subjects. Quaint peasants and street vendors were produced and some classical models as well; decorative pieces included candelabra. In 1782 the factory was sold and production ceased around this time, though there is doubt about the actual date.

# SWITZERLAND

## Zurich (1763–91)

At Schooren, on the Lake of Zurich, a porcelain factory was founded in 1763 by a syndicate whose aims were not only commercial success but the provision of work for local people and the encouragement of national enterprise. The manager was Adam Spengler, whose son later came to England as modeller at Derby. Soft-paste porcelain was made at first, in which steatite was used, but after two years hard-paste was made with kaolin from Lorraine and Limoges. The porcelain tended to be ivory-yellow in colour. At first a Rococo style was used, influenced by a much earlier period of Meissen; later the Neo-classical fashion was followed.

Zurich tea caddy, c. 1767.

Zurich figure group, c. 1770.

All kinds of tableware were made, including decorative table-centres, as well as snuff boxes, toys, candlesticks, cane handles and scent bottles. J-shaped handles were typical of the factory. Decoration was very fine; Gessner specialised in landscapes and scenes from the Dutch masters while other painters were J. H. Bleuler, H. Füssli, and H. Thomann. Transfer printing was also used. Good figures were made, mostly of contemporary genre subjects, but also including sets of the Seasons, Continents, Elements, etc., and models from mythology and the Italian Comedy. Some work in biscuit was done and bases were very simple in the form of a square or pad shape. Chief modeller was J. V. Sonnenschein, who had former- ly worked at Ludwigsburg.

Nyon sprigged cup and saucer,
late eighteenth century.

## Nyon (1781–1813)

At Nyon, on Lake Geneva, a porcelain factory was founded
towards the end of the eighteenth century by Ferdinand
Müller and his son-in-law Jacob Dortu. Both were decorators
who had worked at a number of factories; Müller had been at
Tournai, Nymphenburg and Capodimonte, and Dortu had
worked at Berlin, Cassel, Ansbach and Marieberg and at the
last factory he had been an arcanist. The partnership lasted
five years though other workmen came from Zurich, Lunéville
Ludwigsburg and Sèvres. A good hard-paste porcelain was
made from kaolin brought from Limoges and the factory based
its style mainly on the wares of Sèvres and Paris. The colours
used came from Eisenach. As one would expect of a factory
starting late in the eighteenth century, the prevailing style was
Neo-classical, creating a fine white ware decorated with flowers.

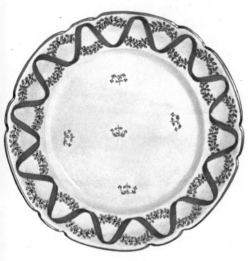

Nyon plate with ribbon decoration.

All kinds of tableware were made but nothing much more adventurous in form than a *trembleuse* cup and saucer, which was not galleried but deeply recessed to hold the cup firm. The handles were square shaped. Etienne Gide, a miniaturist, painted figures in landscape, and a scene of folk watching players from the Italian Comedy performing in an open-air theatre is attributed to him. Work was done *en camaieu* (in tones of the same colour) and in polychrome. The Meissen onion pattern was used and also the Angoulême sprig of cornflowers. Other painters, who were originally at Ludwigs-burg, were Joseph Pernaux and William Rath. Müller left in 1786 and the factory was run for a time by Jean Georges Zinkernagel who borrowed money to rebuild in the Rue de la Porcelaine. In 1787 Dortu, who had gone to Berlin, returned and was in charge of the factory until it closed in 1813.

# DENMARK

## Copenhagen (1759–65)

It is possible that the first attempts to produce porcelain in Denmark were made by the wandering Hunger and Lück from Meissen, but without success. In 1755 another modeller from Meissen, Melhorn, is said to have experimented at the Blaatarn, with kaolin from the island of Bornholm. The earliest porcelain which is authenticated, however, is the soft-paste made by Louis Fournier, a modeller who had worked at Chantilly and at Vincennes. He was brought from France by Frederick V of Denmark and established in a pottery in the Blaatarn. There he produced an excellent porcelain with a yellowish hue, finely decorated and reminiscent of late Chantilly. Elaborate tableware was made in which the *rose Pompadour* ground, mosaic borders and gilt scrollwork were used. Decoration was of scenes from mythology and with swags of flowers in relief.

Copenhagen bowl.

The next factory to produce porcelain in Copenhagen was founded at Købmagergade in 1775 by a chemist, Frantz Heinrich Müller. He had been experimenting since 1771 with the aid of a mining engineer, J. G. von Langen, who had helped Benckgraff in the establishment of the factory at Fürstenberg. By 1774 a company was formed and in 1776 A. C. Luplau, modeller and arcanist from Fürstenberg, was persuaded to come to Denmark and brought with him German workers. Luplau developed the formula for the porcelain, which was hard-paste. The influx of foreign workers included the decorator J. C. Bayer from Nuremberg. The standard of wares was greatly improved but nevertheless the factory found itself in financial difficulties and the king had to lend it his support from 1779. The style of the period was late Rococo showing the influence of Fürstenberg. The three wavy lines adopted as the mark of this period represent the three waterways of Denmark entering the Baltic, the Sound and the Great and Little Belts.

Woman with a chicken, c. 1780.

# Royal Copenhagen Porcelain Manufactory (from 1779)

From the time that the factory became the responsibility of the king it took the Royal prefix. Production was now mainly in the Neo-classical style, its inspiration principally German as one might expect with so many of its workers coming from that country. A task of heroic proportions was taken on at this period in the form of the *Flora Danica* service, which was intended to include 2,500 pieces and was commissioned as a gift for the Empress Catherine II of Russia. Some 1,600 pieces were in fact made, on which were painted specimens of the native flowers of Denmark, as illustrated in a great botanical work which had been published there in 1761. No two pieces were alike and the work progressed for twelve years being carried out mostly by J. C. Bayer, assisted latterly by C. N. Faxöe. The modeller of the fruit and flower baskets was Søren Preuss. In 1802 the Crown Prince put an end to the work on the service, which remained in Denmark. It was the largest service ever to be made by a porcelain factory.

*Flora Danica* plate.

Copenhagen tureen, c. 1785.

Many figures were made at this time, the most popular being the genre pieces, particularly of Norwegian peasants. During the first year of production over thirty different models were designed; in 1781 twenty-seven more were introduced and in 1782 fifty-six figures of Norwegian peasants were among the range of subjects produced. Some of these figures were even available in a variety of sizes. Most other models were based on European originals, and figures in the classical manner were made in biscuit.

A variety of objects were produced: decorative plaques for inlay into furniture, brush backs, mirror frames, buttons, handles, tobacco boxes which were decorated with landscapes, cupids, flowers, birds, fruit, silhouettes and monograms. The factory suffered a setback when it was damaged by British gunfire in 1807.

During the nineteenth century little of importance was produced but in 1884, when Phillip Schon became director, with Arnold Krog in charge of the Art Department, the factory removed to Smallgarde, Fredericksberg, and once more work of interest was done, with the emphasis on fine glazes.

Buen Retiro holy water stoup.

## SPAIN

### Buen Retiro (1759–1808)

In 1759 Charles acceded to the throne of Spain and left Naples taking with him the complete factory of Capodimonte, including Gaetano Schepers and his son Carlos, his workmen, materials, moulds and models. He set up a factory at Buen Retiro near Madrid and the use of an identical paste and the same mark make the early wares indistinguishable from those of Capodimonte. One of the first commissions to be executed by the new factory was a porcelain room for the Palace of Aranjuez, after the one left behind at Portici. Until the beginning of the new century pieces made were mainly decorative and often on a big scale. Supports for tables, holy water stoups, chandeliers, mirror frames, plaques, ewers and basins were typical products, as were small figure groups, figures supporting candlesticks, cherubs, genre pieces, classical and religious subjects. From 1770 to 1783 Carlos Schepers encountered some difficulties with the paste, of which he was in charge and which was extremely yellow with the glaze not well wedded to the body. At the end of the century, in the hands of Carlos Gricci, a better porcelain was produced.

## Alcora

Alcora figure of Winter, c. 1775.

The precise date of the founding of the factory at Alcora, near Valencia, is not known, but it was certainly some time in the mid eighteenth century. Its founder was a politician, Count Aranda, who was Prime Minister during the reign of Charles III. It was his ambition for Alcora that it should become world renowned for its porcelain, but in fact it is not widely known. It may be said of the Count, in passing, that he protested strongly against the cruelty of bull-fighting and appears to have been a man out of his time. A Frenchman named Ollery, who had formerly worked at Moustiers, was in charge of the factory and the form of the wares was after the French style. Tableware and domestic pieces were made, decorated in bright colours, blue and yellow being a favoured combination, and greens and mauves were often used. Rich ground colours were applied in which medallions were left for flower painting. Figures were made, their subject matter drawn from rustic life and from mythology, and were generally left uncoloured. A life-size bust of the founder was made in polychrome.

# AMERICA

There is some evidence to suggest that experiments in the making of porcelain took place in Virginia as early as 1745. In this year William Cookworthy of Plymouth, England, referred in a letter to the manufacturer of 'Chinaware' in Virginia and imported some of the clay used there for experiments of his own. There are no records, however, of the potteries which made it.

## Bonin and Morris (1770–74)

About 1770 a factory was established at Prime St Southwark near Schulkill Permanent Bridge, by Gousse Bonin, of French or Flemish origin but coming from the English factory of Bow. The company advertised widely for skilled workmen in England and brought many over to America. Large amounts of bone ash were included in the paste and wares closely followed the style of Bow. Both white and coloured wares were made. It was not till 1825 that porcelain emerged from the experimental stage when, at an already established pottery, porcelain was produced by what was then styled the Jersey City Porcelain and Earthenware Co., where most of the workers were of French origin. The body was a hard-paste porcelain decorated mainly in gold, but the competition from English wares proved too much for the American manufacturers and by 1828 they were closing down.

Bonin & Morris basket, c. 1742.

Tucker pedestal vase,
c. 1830.

## Tucker and Hulme (1826–38)

Originally a porcelain decorator, William Ellis Tucker experimented with local clays and, joined later by Thomas Hulme, produced a hard-paste porcelain with a good glaze. Early tablewares were clumsily decorated with flowers, insects and landscapes in sepia. White wares were made sometimes decorated with gilt bands, and polychrome paintings were done of fruit and flowers.

## Fenton

In 1847 C. W. Fenton began to manufacture porcelain at Bennington in Vermont. Hard-paste biscuit was generally decorated in white relief against a coloured ground; quality varied a great deal.

(*left*) Goss platter, c. 1870.
(*right*) Bust of the founder.

## MISCELLANEOUS PORCELAIN

### Goss (1858–1929)

By the nineteenth century porcelain was no longer a rare and precious material. A variety of fine pastes were being mass-produced for the flourishing bourgeoisie and eye-catching opulence was more appreciated than aesthetics. A few of the factories producing finer wares have been included in this book, but it is not on grounds of quality that Goss is mentioned here, but because it was a phenomenon whose history traces the change from supplying a good standard porcelain at a reasonable price, to creating and benefiting from a popular craze for collecting. William Henry Goss started his career as chief artist and designer for Copelands. He founded his own factory, the Falcon Works at Stoke-on-Trent, in 1858, where he produced Parian ware and also a glazed Parian known as Ivory Porcelain. The latter brought him an award for the best work in this medium at the International Exhibition held in London in 1862. Among many pieces treated in a similar way, he showed an elaborate comport, pierced, moulded, gilded and bejewelled with solid gems of enamel which were said to be cut and polished and to be far finer than the jewelled wares of Sèvres. All manner of items were made, in the florid taste of the times, but with impeccable craftsmanship.

In 1880 Goss was joined by his son Adolphus William Henry and it was most probably due to this young man that a completely new line of porcelain was tried on the market. This was the Heraldic Ware, which proved such a success that, although other forms of porcelain continued to be made, the main production of the factory was devoted to it. Among the first examples of the new pieces were designs to commemorate the Golden Jubilee of Queen Victoria in 1887. The Imperial Crown was set over a V for Victoria inside the Garter Star on some; on others the national emblems were used. The success of these led to further issues on royal occasions. The local authorities of various towns, cities and boroughs of note were then approached for their permission to use the coats of arms of their towns and cities on pieces of porcelain. It was decided that this ware should be made in the form of some object of local interest. The great revolution in modes of travel at this time was developing an ever increasing tourist trade. The wares found an immediate market and the souvenir business began in a big way. It was to expand till the factory was exporting its wares all over the world and only the outbreak of the First World War checked its progress. Other selling lines were introduced during the period from 1880, none of which had any artistic merit. Decoration did not enhance form and the form was only considered for what it represented.

## Miscellaneous Collectors' Pieces

Apart from the fine porcelain of the eighteenth and nineteenth centuries there are many pieces which have found favour in the eyes of collectors. Nostalgia plays a great part, and porcelain of no great aesthetic merit, produced for a mass market, acquires a historical significance in time. Even the more serious collector may have a corner set apart for a few trivialities which now come under the heading of bygones, some of which have even been paid the compliment recently of being reproduced. Most of the pieces could have been found on cottage shelves or the mantelpieces of seaside boarding houses before the Second World War. Superior to these, however, are the models hitherto attributed to Rockingham, and here put in their place as Staffordshire. There are charming cottages which usually serve as pastille burners; sometimes the roof is removeable, sometimes the house comes off the base, or there is an entrance left at the back to poke the pastille through. Little French poodles, sometimes with baskets of flowers in their mouths, have long been favourites; a mother dog and pups is less common. A number of simply modelled, naive, but charming figures were made, one type having broad-brimmed hats, turned back and gilded underneath with a soft gold. Children with animals and a boy riding on a dog are among the pieces to be found. Dogs predominate over cats.

Staffordshire poodle.

Recently a fashionable form of china to collect has been the more elegant pieces of gilt and white ware, particularly of creamers and coffee cans, and the same articles in polychrome are equally popular. Straight-sided coffee cans have the advantage of looking complete without their saucers; tea cups are less obliging. Porcelain tulips, of which Spode did some particularly splendid examples, are increasingly collected. Plaques are also sought after but examples of both types are hard to come by.

Teapots provide rather a wider field and some good examples can be picked up very cheaply if one is prepared to accept star cracks in the base which confine them to display only. The line is easily spoiled by damage to spouts and handles. There emerges a surprising variety of shapes in which a teapot can be designed, including the Cadogan teapot which fills at the base, and there were many ingenious devices in the nineteenth century for trapping the leaves and keeping the tea warm.

Mugs lend themselves to the forming of an interesting collection, for most historic occasions have been celebrated by the issuing of commemoration mugs. Apart from these they range from the elegance of Swansea and Derby to the charm of Victorian pieces made for children. There is also a wide variety of sizes from miniature to pint-sized.

Gilt and white coffee can (Worcester).

Hand vase and Meissen spittoon.

Cats and birds of course have always been popular subjects, and swans had a particular vogue recently. Shoes that used to be seen so often, stuffed with velvet to hold pins, are fast disappearing on to collectors' shelves. Subject matter plays an important part and pieces which have something to do with cricket, boxing, racing, or any sport in its early stages, are valued far beyond their worth as porcelain. Miniatures have always held a fascination and many factories have produced toys such as tiny chairs and tables, minute trays holding tea services, little pots of flowers and so on. Victorian scent bottles offer a charming variety, and shells are a subject which can take a great many forms and have eternal appeal. Decorative plates to hang on the wall are now quite difficult to find. Medical pieces of all kinds are much collected, which include eye baths, male and female bed bottles, spittoons, invalid feeders, dosing spoons and babies' pap bottles. Their unfamiliar shapes, which are often of great beauty, tend to override any consideration of their original purposes. They are more readily found in blue and white and therefore the rarer pieces in polychrome are greatly in demand.

A great variety of gift china was made for the holiday trade, marked with 'A present from Brighton' or some other suitable inscription. The tradition of souvenir china goes back to the eighteenth century, such as the 'Trifle from Lowestoft'. Strangely enough this remunerative trade was not, in the nineteenth century, dominated by English factories but was to a great extent supplied by Germany. First among these factories was Springer and Oppenheimer who, between 1860 and 1890, were solely responsible for a particular type of figure group made in a heavy white hard-paste with a thick glaze. These were called fairings but were not made merely to be won at a coconut shy; they had a broad humour comparable to the sea-side postcard, and were bought as presents for the 'folks at home'. They might be thought of as 'bed pieces', as a popular subject was 'Last in bed puts out the light', although the majority of groups did not in fact include a bed. A few titles give the general idea of the scene enacted: 'Returning home at one o'clock in the morning', 'Kiss me quick', 'The landlord in love' etc. They have a few touches of colour, and a gold line about the base. Pieces include street vendors, subjects connected with the Franco-Prussian war, sentimental groups of children and animals in human dress.

Springer &
Oppenheimer souvenir piece.

Samson imitation of a *famille rose* Chinese mug.

## REPRODUCTIONS, FAKES AND FORGERIES

Fine pieces made in an earlier age have always been a challenge to the craftsman, and copies have not always been made with intention of deceiving. In the case of the Chinese, reign marks were sometimes added to pay tribute to the original design. There was never a period in Chinese porcelain in which work was not also done in an earlier style, and so great was the skill of the potters that only with great familiarity with authentic pieces is it possible to identify them. In the nineteenth century many European factories reproduced pieces from the previous century by using old moulds. These can best be detected by the overglaze, the colouring of which tends to be influenced by nineteenth-century taste. The painting is usually arbitrary and does not stand up to close scrutiny. The factories of Nantgarw and Minton made excellent reproductions of Sèvres, which were, however, properly marked. The early Derby factory closely followed the style of Chelsea to the extent of adding the anchor mark before the factories combined. Doccia reproduced its early pieces and, using old moulds bought from Capodimonte, made quantities of porcelain which had been produced only in small quantities originally.

(*above*) Chinese imitation of a
Sung pot.
(*right*) Samson copy of a
Sèvres bisque figure.

The necessity of replacing damaged pieces from time to
time led to the making of replicas by many factories. At the
end of the eighteenth century Derby was making replacements
of Meissen and Fürstenberg, to which the original mark was
added, and a replacement service was run by Mason of Fentons
in 1804. The use of marks as a guide to authenticity is very
unreliable as, ever since they were first used, they were
pirated by other factories both at home and abroad, and forgery
was widespread from the eighteenth century onwards. The
German factories were well marked, and so was Sèvres; on the
other hand English porcelain was not. Copies of early soft-paste
porcelain are easiest to detect since replicas are generally in
hard-paste which is easier to handle, though the Tournai
copies of Chelsea are an exception to this rule. In the time of
Yung-chêng many copies were made of Sung porcelain which
were honestly marked, but some of the marks have been removed at a later date. Samson of Paris, working from 1845,
advertised that he produced 'Reproductions of Ancient Works
emanating from the Museums and from private collections',
but asserted that an S was added to the original mark of the
object copied. This addition, if it was really used consistently,
is now missing in most cases.

It is a relatively simple matter to remove an overglaze mark with acid, but it usually leaves a tell-tale dullness on the glaze. Samson produced a great deal of Chinese armorial ware, and frequently pieces which are claimed to be Chinese Lowestoft proved to be neither Chinese nor Lowestoft but Samson reproductions. There is a certain cold, hard colour about these pieces which is not difficult for an expert to recognise, but some excellent copies were made of Meissen figures. It is in the overglaze that they mostly give themselves away; the fine painting of the hair with minute brush strokes is absent, the balance of colour is not exact and the enamel does not marry quite so well with the glaze. The century of its origin is indefinably apparent. In the late nineteenth century, Helena Wolfsohn of Dresden, a manufacturer of porcelain and a decorator of Meissen wares, purchased in the white, added the A R mark to pieces indiscriminately. About 1880 an injunction was brought against her and the practice was stopped. There have been several studio potters who have been tempted to test their craftsmanship on an occasional reproduction, and as these were probably made with something like the original formula it needs a connoisseur to identify them.

Saucer marked A R by Helena Wolfsohn.

Fake Chelsea tureen.

There are many fakes of Chelsea tureens in the form of cabbages or bundles of asparagus, as well as pieces in the form of tulips. It must be emphasized that familiarity with the genuine articles enables most of these to be detected at a glance. Even in first rate reproductions there is a deadness, perhaps due to over-meticulousness, not present in the original. The most difficult forgeries to detect are those where original undecorated pieces have been enamelled expertly at a later date, or slightly decorated pieces have been enhanced. Reproduction can become very involved, as in Chinese copies of European ware copying the Chinese! At the present time the market is flooded with cheap reproductions of the less important nineteenth-century wares, such as the so-called Rockingham figures and Staffordshire china. Careful examination should expose the deception. The most obvious aspect to examine is the gold since it is now very difficult to achieve a good gold overglaze, which is generally bright and brassy and often has a stain of purple spreading into the glaze. Dirt and wear are painstakingly added and the inside of a pastille burner has even been known to have had the black of smoke fired on! All for the sake of authenticity.

A typical restoration problem.

## RESTORATION

The restorations of broken ceramics is by no means a new idea; the Chinese at an early date camouflaged cracks and chips with gold inlay which was aesthetically most pleasing and they bound damaged rims with metals. In a type of restoration, the eighteenth-century European factories rescued pieces marred in the firing by painting over the blemishes. With the greatly increased interest in antique porcelain, that which still survives will be spread more thinly among the collectors, and it is obvious that the age and fragility of the material make it impossible to demand that every piece should be undamaged. *Bocage*, finger tips, plumes of hats, the tails and ears of animals and other projections are the usual parts which have come to grief through the years of dusting and washing, but if all parts of a figure exist and are assembled without unsightly blemish, a piece can be broken into several parts without visual loss. With flatwares, plates and dishes, etc., the effect is less easy to disguise without camouflaging restoration.

A very fine collection of representative porcelain can be acquired by the amateur at little cost if he is willing to take damaged pieces. There is no better way of familiarising oneself with really good pieces without risking a costly mistake and, if it proves to be an exceptionally good buy, the cost of restoration may well be worthwhile. Restoration is not, however, a job for the amateur or for the china mender who is used to dealing with commonplace domestic breakages mostly requiring rivetting. I have seen fine pieces with holes bored in the stumps of arms and legs to take a peg to make a join secure, and even found figures with limbs ground to fit on again when a connecting chip has been missing. A restorer of fine porcelain should be able to make up missing parts and camouflage unsightly joins and a few are capable of fine modelling and can remake a missing limb in porcelain after having consulted an original figure. Although picture restoration has been an accepted craft for centuries, china restoration has only become one since the availability of durable materials. It has been claimed by some restorers that it is possible to make a piece whole again by firing broken parts on to the body. Since clay will not fuse together once it has been fired, such a claim must be unfounded; glaze might hold it together but, as its fusing point is much higher than that of enamel colours, the latter would inevitably be damaged in the process. Any applied gold would be burnt off even earlier at a lower temperature. When a piece is refired, for the purpose of touching up the enamel or reglazing, the usual result is a bubbling and black pitting over the surface.

It may indeed be possible to obtain a glaze with a very low firing temperature, but apart from the great difficulty of balancing the piece in position during the repair operation, the new glaze acting as an adhesive would still leave a scar around the break which would need to be camouflaged before a perfect and invisible restoration was achieved. This is a delicate operation that requires both experience and expertise.

# BIBLIOGRAPHY

*Early American Pottery and China* by John Spargo. New York, 1926.

*Notes on American Ceramics 1607–1943* by Arthur W. Clement. Handbook to the Museum Collections, Brooklyn Museum, Brooklyn, 1964.

*China Collecting in America* by E. M. Earle. New York, 1892; New edition, New York, 1924.

*Anglo-American China*, Parts I & II, by Sam Laidacker. Bristol, Pa., 1951.

*Early Chinese Pottery and Porcelain* by Basil Gray, London, 1953.

*Concise Encyclopedia of English Pottery and Porcelain* by Wolf Mankowitz and Reginald Haggar. London and New York, 1957.

*Chinese Pottery and Porcelain* (2 vols) by R. L. Hobson. London, 1950.

*Ceramic Art of China* by W. B. Honey. London, 1945.

*Chinese Export Art in the Eighteenth Century* by Margaret Jourdain and Soame Jenyns. London, 1950.

*Royal Copenhagen Porcelain* by A. Hayden. London, 1911.

*The Ceramic Art of Great Britain* (2 vols) by Llewellyn Jewitt. London, 1878.

*British Pottery Marks* by G. W. Rhead. London, 1910.

*English Pottery and Porcelain* by W. B. Honey. 3rd ed., London, 1947.

*Nineteenth Century English Pottery and Porcelain* by G. Bembrose. London, 1952.

*Wedgwood Ware* by W. B. Honey. London, 1948.

*English Porcelain Figures of the Eighteenth Century* by W. King. London, 1925.

*English Blue and White Porcelain of the Eighteenth Century* by J. L. Dixon. London, 1952.

*Old English Porcelain* by G. Savage. London, 1952.

*English Porcelain of the Eighteenth Century* by J. L. Dixon. London, 1952.

*Eighteenth Century English Porcelain* by G. Savage. London, 1952.

*Dresden China* by W. B. Honey. London, 1934 and 1946.

*European Ceramic Art* by W. B. Honey. London, 1949.

*Le Porcellane di Capodimonte* by Barone Angelo de Eisner Eisenhof. Milan, 1925.

*World Ceramics,* edited by R. J. Charleston. London, 1968.

# INDEX

## OTHER TITLES
## IN THE SERIES